CHRIST
THE LORD

THE AYER LECTURESHIP was founded in May, 1928, in the Rochester Theological Seminary, by the gift of twenty-five thousand dollars from Mr. and Mrs. Wilfred W. Fry, of Camden, New Jersey, to perpetuate the memory of Mrs. Fry's father, the late Mr. Francis Wayland Ayer. At the time of his death, Mr. Ayer was president of the corporation which maintained the Rochester Theological Seminary.

Shortly after the establishment of the lectureship, the Rochester Theological Seminary and the Colgate Theological Seminary were united under the name of the Colgate-Rochester Divinity School. It is under the auspices of this institution that the Ayer lectures are given.

Under the terms of the foundation, the lectures are to fall under the broad field of the history of interpretation of the Christian religion and message. It is the desire of those connected with the establishment and the administration of the lectureship that the lectures shall be religiously constructive, and shall help in the building of Christian faith.

Four lectures are to be given each year at the Colgate-Rochester Divinity School at Rochester, New York, and these lectures are to be published in book form within one year after the time of their delivery. They will be known as the Ayer Lectures.

Books by the Same Author

" He Whom a Dream Hath Possessed," 1932
Philemon Among the Letters of Paul, 1935
The Man Christ Jesus, 1941
Marcion and the New Testament, 1942
Religion and the Present Crisis (editor) , 1942

CHRIST
THE LORD

THE MEANING OF JESUS
IN THE EARLY CHURCH

By JOHN KNOX

WILLETT, CLARK & COMPANY
CHICAGO   NEW YORK
1945

To John

ἀγαπητὸν . . . καὶ ἐν σαρκὶ καὶ ἐν κυρίῳ

Foreword

THIS BOOK comprises the lectures it was my privilege to give at the Colgate-Rochester Divinity School in April of 1944 on the Ayer Foundation. Except that only four of the six lectures could be actually delivered and that footnotes and a bibliography have been added, the book does hardly more than present in printed form the lectures as they were spoken. Little has been done to alter their form and style and no attempt has been made to conceal their original character.

The book presumes to be no more than an introduction to its theme. It is in no way a systematic presentation of New Testament Christology. Only a few topics from a wide field are selected for discussion, and the author is painfully aware of important omissions. Limitations of time, as well as of learning and understanding, made this selective procedure inevitable. In a way this book is a kind of sequel to my *The Man Christ Jesus* — an attempt, partly, to fill in and, partly, to enlarge somewhat the picture which that small book presents. I have as carefully as possible avoided repetition, which means that a few things I should certainly have wanted to say in this book are not said because they were said in that.

I am grateful to the president and members of the faculty of the Colgate-Rochester Divinity School for their many courtesies to me during the period of the lectures and for the honor they conferred on me in asking me to give them. And I shall always gratefully remember the students, alumni and others attending the convocation for their unfailing patience and kindness.

It would be impossible adequately to acknowledge my obligation to many friends and colleagues, but I want especially to mention Professor Frederick C. Grant and Professor Francis W. Beare, who have assisted me at many points in the preparation of this book.

JOHN KNOX

New York

Contents

Part One

He Was Remembered

Lecture 1

THE TITLE I have ventured to propose for these lectures is an ambitious one, for at its widest it covers the whole content of the New Testament. Paul reminds the church at Corinth that when he was with them he had preached nothing except Jesus; a glance at the New Testament will indicate that Paul was not alone in this preoccupation. The faith and the life of the early church were centered about Jesus, and one could not speak without using his name. That name occurs a thousand times in the New Testament, and if separate references to " Christ " and " the Lord " were included, the count would be even higher — indeed, much higher. Nor are these occurrences confined to the Gospels, where Jesus' life and teaching are being explicitly described; they are to be found almost as frequently in the Epistles — and in all manner of connections. Paul's little note to Philemon, for example, hardly more than a page long and concerned largely with an owner's relations with a slave, refers to Jesus as many as ten times. The meaning of Jesus in the early church is nothing less than the whole meaning of the whole New Testament. It is even more than that, for it is the meaning of the life of the early church itself.

The word " meaning," as we ordinarily use it, has two senses: one abstract, the other concrete; one formulable in terms of ideas, the other even partly expressible only in terms of art or action. In the first sense " meaning " is truth understood; in the second it is reality experienced. One may ask, for example, what is the meaning of the war which at this moment has engulfed the world, and answer with an explanation of why the war occurred, of what is happening in it, and of what is to be expected from it. But one may ask the same question and know that the answer can never be given in words. The meaning of the war in this second sense is the actual impact of the war on the millions who are involved in it. It is the anguish of waiting, the agony of struggle; it is killing and being killed, maiming and being maimed; it is leave-taking, absence, fear and hope, joy and despair, devotion and hatred, escape and death; it is the exultation of victory; it is the bitterness of defeat; it is the incalculable aggregate of all the blood, sweat, and tears the war is costing the thousands who fight and the millions who suffer the war's desolation. The meaning of the war in this sense is what the war is actually doing to the minds, hearts, consciences, and bodies of men and women. That meaning cannot be expressed in conceptual terms. It cannot be expressed at all, in the way an idea can be expressed. The best words can do is to represent, stand for, point out, symbolize or suggest this kind of meaning; they cannot contain it. Great works of art are all concerned with meaning in this concrete sense.

Now when we speak of the meaning of Jesus in the early church, we have both of these senses in mind. We are thinking both of what he actually was and of the ways in which he was understood and interpreted. We are thinking both of the concrete impact of Jesus upon the members of the community which was formed about him and of the ways in which the community tried to explain the magnitude and the revolutionary consequences of that impact. We are thus concerned with both Christ and Christology, with both life and dogma.

Of these two concerns there can be no question as to which is more important: life is more important than dogma, Christ than Christology. Christianity grew out of an event, or, better perhaps, a closely knit series of events; it was not the elaboration of an abstract idea or ideal. That event, or the center of that series of events, was the person whom we know as Jesus Christ. All distinctively and authentically Christian ideas are inferences from " the thing that has happened among us," are attempts to explain and interpret it. But although there can be no question that in the last analysis fact is more important than explanation, actually they cannot be separated, for some measure of explanation and interpretation — adequate or inadequate, accurate or inaccurate — is part and parcel of any knowledge of objective reality it is given us to have. If there is such a thing as a " bare fact," certainly we cannot know one. If there is such a thing as a merely objective event, certainly we can have no knowledge of it as such. History and interpretation, distinguishable in idea, cannot in fact be separated.

The false assumption that they can be separated and that a purely objective historiography is possible (or could be true even if it were possible) partly accounts for the dryness, unreality, and irrelevance which have sometimes characterized biblical scholarship. For a generation or more biblical scholarship has been committed to what is known as the historical method — that is, to the aim of seeing the books of the Bible in their historical setting and understanding them as nearly as possible in the way their writers and first readers understood them. · This historical method of interpretation stands over against the modernizing method, which makes the words of the Scripture mean whatever they may happen to mean to the naïve contemporary reader. The distinction between these two methods is manifest, real, and important.

But as much as this cannot be said for another distinction, of which one often hears, between the historical interpretation of the Bible on the one hand, and an interpretation variously called devotional, religious, or theological, on the other. This distinction is often drawn in theory and is constantly exemplified in practice, but it is a false and vicious distinction. There can be no true religious or devotional or theological understanding of the Bible which is not also historical understanding. Once we cut loose from the historical sense of the Bible, we have cut loose from the Bible, although we may play all kinds of homiletical games with its words. This, I hope, is clear enough, although what interpreter with a practical religious interest is altogether free from guilt in this matter?

What is not so clear, but is equally true, is that there can be no true historical understanding of the Bible which is not also devotional, or religious, or theological. For the books of the Bible are not primarily concerned with facts in some hypothetical " bare " sense, but with meanings in the concrete sense of the term. Now such meanings cannot be apprehended with the same kind and degree of objectivity as formal facts can be. One cannot understand such meanings from the outside; one must see them from within. This involves the likelihood, perhaps the necessity, of subjective mistakes; but that risk must be taken, although only with all possible caution. The historian who steadfastly keeps himself as a person out of his study of an epoch may avoid certain subjective errors, but he misses most of the epoch. Purely objective historiography would be neither truly objective nor history. Historiography has to be somewhat subjective in order to be as objective as it can be. This is true because the *objects* of historical study are events, which are in no small part *subjective* objects; for events do not simply happen, as in a vacuum: they happen in connection with persons — they happen not only among persons and to persons, but also in considerable measure within persons — and only persons as persons can even begin to understand what any historical event in its concreteness is. The true historian is artist and philosopher, not scientist only. A good piece of historical writing is a picture, not a map; a living body, not a diagram; a full-length portrait in color, not a list of dimensions or a thumbnail description.

Now what we have in the New Testament is the account of an event, Jesus Christ, as that event occurred — that is, as it was experienced, responded to, became effective — in the community of his followers and their immediate successors. If by the historical study of the New Testament we mean the attempt really to understand that event as it was, then it is clear that no mastery of the critical tools of his craft can be of any but the meagerest use unless the historian stands imaginatively within the event, himself feels the force of it, sees it, as far as may be, as those saw it to whom it first occurred. A cold, dispassionate study of the mightiest event in human history, whatever else it is, cannot be truly and fully historical. It may be accurate, but it is hopelessly inadequate. It may miss being false at any particular point, but it misses being true altogether.

But New Testament study has sometimes been thus cold and dispassionate — has indeed regarded such detachment as a virtue. Detachment *is* a virtue so long as it is not actual separation from the object one is trying to understand. When scholarly detachment means a breaking of concrete contact with the reality the scholar is presumably studying, it defeats itself. One has become so objective that one has lost the object. It is partly because of this self-defeating worship of a false and impossible objectivity that New Testament study has sometimes lost contact with the real life of the ancient church and therefore with the life of the continuing church.

We cannot know the meaning of Jesus in the early church except as we know what he actually was within the experience of the men and women who formed the community. To say this is to say that the New Testament does not belong to secular scholarship. Secular scholarship can make immense contributions to the understanding of the New Testament, but cannot itself understand even the first word of it. The New Testament belongs to the church. The church wrote it; only the church can read it. I am not referring here to any magical qualification; the secular scholarship which succeeded in understanding the New Testament would, by that token, have become Christian scholarship. To know the concrete meaning of Jesus in the early church is to belong to the Christian community, for only within the community did the meaning first exist and only within the community has it been conveyed to us. One who finds it at all finds it there. Indeed, might it not be said that a knowledge of this meaning of Jesus is and has always been constitutive of membership in the Christian community?

A very few words will indicate the procedure we expect to follow in these lectures. A visitor at one of the meetings of a typical church at the middle of the first century, hearing the name of Jesus spoken again and again, would, I believe, have received three impressions: he would have gathered that Jesus was a person remembered; that he was a person still known as a living reality by the members of the group; and that he was a person about whom certain important theological ideas were held. A reader coming fresh to the New Testament would get this same threefold impression: Jesus was for its writers an object of memory, of present experience, and of theological reflection. These lectures will attempt as much elaboration of this impression as limitations of time will permit:

" He was remembered," " He was known still," " He was interpreted." The remainder of this and the following two lectures will be devoted to the first of these topics; the fourth lecture, to the second topic; and the final two, to the third. It must not be forgotten that the three topics, differentiated from one another for purposes of discussion, represent aspects of one unified meaning, and that actually memory, religious faith, and theology were fused indissolubly. Although I shall occasionally refer to other sections of the New Testament and to extracanonical literature, we shall rely chiefly upon Paul and the Gospels as constituting the most important witnesses to the meaning of Jesus in the early church.

The earliest books of the New Testament are the letters of Paul. These letters were written over a span of not more than twenty years just before and after the middle of the first century and therefore within what might be called the first Christian generation. They had all been written and Paul himself had died before the earliest Gospel was written, and they had been assembled and published and were in wide use among the churches before the last of the Gospels was composed.

This Pauline collection contained ten letters. One of these, the Epistle to the Ephesians, was probably composed, after Paul's own time, by a disciple well acquainted with the apostle's writings, perhaps by the collector himself; but the other letters were almost certainly his. Colossians and II Thessalonians are the only letters whose authenticity has even been seriously questioned, and both of them could be surrendered without great loss so far as our understanding of Paul is concerned. That understanding really rests upon Romans, Galatians, Philippians, and the Corinthian letters, all of them undoubtedly genuine. The so-called Pastoral Epistles, I and II Timothy, and Titus, belong to the second century and were not a part of the original collection of Paul's works.[1]

I have already quoted Paul as saying that he was determined to know nothing except Jesus; and one has only to leaf through his letters to see how completely his religious life and thought were dominated by him whom he variously calls " Christ," " Jesus Christ," "the Lord Jesus Christ," or simply " the Lord." Jesus appears most often in Paul's letters as a mighty personal reality known in his own present experience, whose meaning he seeks to interpret; and for that reason Paul will come in for more thorough discussion in the last three lectures in this series. But it cannot be escaped that when Paul speaks of Jesus, he is speaking of a person remembered. The reality which he knows so intimately and surely and whose meaning he can explain only in the most exalted theological terms is a man who walked the earth not long ago and whom hundreds of living men vividly recall.

This fact, one may remark in passing, in no small part accounts for the unique power of the Christian message as Paul preached it in a world which, as he is said to have remarked to an audience in Athens, was very religious. Early Christianity is often compared with the mystery cults, which, arising in the East, so strongly appealed to the mind and mood of the West during this period. There were gods many and lords many. There were Serapis, Isis, Mithra, Adonis, Demeter, and many more — all of them addressed as Lord or by some similar title and worshiped as divine. But these were not historical persons actually remembered.

[1] The conclusions thus summarily stated cannot be defended in this book. They rest upon data presented in any good " Introduction " to the New Testament, and (except for some dissent about Ephesians) would be concurred in by virtually all students of the New Testament.

Among the many differences which set a wide gulf between early Christianity and the mysteries, despite many similarities and doubtless no little mutual interpenetration, none was more important than this.[2] It was the memory of a particular man — or, better, it was the particular man himself who was remembered — which, more than any other single factor, gave the Christian community its character and the Christian faith its power. This memory unmistakably underlies Paul's knowledge of Christ and is presupposed in every reference he makes to him. " The Lord Christ " is no vague mythological personage: *Jesus was Lord.*

That this was true for Paul does not depend upon any conclusion one may reach on the question whether Paul had ever seen Jesus in the flesh.[3] That question is unimportant. If Paul had seen Jesus, he certainly had no more than merely seen him. If he knew him, he knew him only

[2] For an excellent discussion of the mystery cults see S. J. Case, *The Evolution of Early Christianity* (Chicago: University of Chicago Press, 1914) , pp. 284 ff. This chapter refers to most of the important literature on the subject. Of general books in English appearing later than 1914 the most valuable is probably H. R. Willoughby, *Pagan Regeneration* (Chicago: University of Chicago Press, 1929) .

[3] This question has been vigorously discussed, frequently in connection with the larger question of how real and close was Jesus' influence upon Paul, a question of which, as I am now endeavoring to point out, it is really independent. On the whole, I should be inclined to say that Paul had not been acquainted with Jesus (in spite of the apparent, but not necessary, implication of II Cor. 5:16) . But on the other side see J. Weiss. *Paul and Jesus* (London and New York: Harper & Brothers, 1909) . May I say, however, that Weiss's principal argument seems to me to involve a curious error? This argument is that Paul could not have recognized as Jesus the glorious figure which, according to Acts, appeared to him in his vision on the Damascus road, if he had not already had in his mind such a picture of Jesus as could have been gained only by actual sight. But is it not a fact that we often, perhaps usually, have in our minds an impression of the appearance of any person about whom we have thought or heard much, even though we may have had no actual basis for the impression, either in our own experience or in what others have told us? How often we say when we meet a person about whom we have heard others speak: " You do not look in the least like the person I had expected to see."

in the way Pilate or the high priest knew him, and therefore did not know him at all. Paul's effective knowledge
of Jesus came to him only after Jesus' crucifixion, by way
of the testimony of others. He entered into the shared remembrance of Jesus which lay, has always lain, and lies
still, near the center of the life of the Christian community.

To the reality and importance of this shared remembrance the very existence of the Gospels bears witness. It is
often pointed out that the four Gospels — especially the
historically most valuable of them, the first three Gospels
— are not personal compositions in nearly so important a
sense as they are creations of the early church. The Gospels are community books. They were composed not by
historians, with what we like to call scientific detachment,
but by Christian preachers and teachers, and for certain
practical purposes. It is undoubtedly true, as we shall frequently have occasion to observe in these lectures, that the
Gospels reflect the interests and are addressed to the felt
needs of Gentile churches in the late first and early second
centuries. These interests and needs were many and di-
verse, and it is not difficult to show that they often func-
tioned to determine not only the selection of materials a
Gospel writer used but also the precise form in which he
presented them. But one of these interests — and surely
not the least important of them — was simply an interest
in remembering Jesus as he was. Papias, an important
Christian teacher of Hierapolis about 150 A.D., tells us with
what eagerness he listened to anyone who had talked with
one of the apostles and who could therefore bring him
some fresh memory of Jesus.[4] Who can doubt that, however many other interests operated to produce the Gospels,

---

[4] This appears in the preface of Papias' work, *Exposition of the Oracles
of the Lord*, as quoted by Eusebius, *Ecclesiastical History*, iii, 39.

this interest in preserving the remembrance of Jesus was one of the most powerful of them?

But if this can be said of the Gospels, it is much more clearly true of the earlier tradition upon which the Gospel writers depended. For the Gospels, especially the first three, are community books not only in the sense that they reflect the interests and needs of the community, but also because they put into what proved to be final form the materials of mixed reminiscence and interpretation of Jesus which had accumulated and circulated among the churches immediately following his career. There is no such thing as pure reminiscence — that is, reminiscence altogether without interpretation — but can we doubt that the Gospel-making process began with the act of remembering, as simply as possible, what Jesus had been, what he had said and done, what had happened to him? Those materials which had proved most useful in preaching and teaching were the items which were finally preserved in the Gospels; but it was often the case that these particular items proved most useful for the same reason they had proved most memorable: they were intrinsically most significant. In the beginning a word or act of Jesus would have been remembered simply because of this significance; only later would its use in preaching and teaching disclose its practical effectiveness.

Apparently an early way of citing a saying of Jesus was with the words: " Remember the words of the Lord Jesus how he said . . ." This formula occurs in the book of Acts and traces of it are to be found in I Clement, Polycarp, and elsewhere.[5] Does not the exhortation " remember " almost certainly go back to the simple question, " Do you remember? " How often that question must have been asked as the first disciples and friends of Jesus met after his

---

[5] See Acts 20:35; I Clement 13:1; Polycarp 2:3.

passion. Then, at least, they must have met largely in remembrance of him. To be sure, they knew him as risen
and they awaited his return; but the significance and power
of this faith and expectation lay in the fact that it was *he*
who had risen and *he* who would come again. They believed because they remembered; memory supported faith
and made it significant. If I may adapt Paul's words to an
unintended use, Jesus in the early church was the object of
faith, hope and love; but here, too, love was " the greatest
of these," because both faith and hope rested firmly upon it
and derived their character from it. Faith and hope might
have neglected the memory of Jesus; love most surely would
not. Love most surely *did* not.

But what was remembered? What was the content of
this original memory of Jesus? That it included much
which is not to be found in our Gospels goes without saying: only the most significant acts and words would continue to be remembered and would thus be accessible to the
Gospel writers a generation or so later. But what about the
materials which our Gospels *do* contain? Did they belong to
the primitive tradition? We recognize that " many other
signs did Jesus in the presence of his disciples which are not
written " [6] in these books; but to what extent can we trust
the things that *are* written there?

The obvious answer here is that whereas the Gospels rest
firmly upon the primitive authentic memory of Jesus, they
contain much which did not belong to that memory. It
was inevitable that this should be true. Recollections were
not immediately written down, or if they were, such early
writings were soon lost or had small circulation. The
stories about Jesus and the reports of his sayings for the

[6] John 20:30.

most part passed by word of mouth from ear to ear, from group to group, in the expanding church, and would suffer some unintentional modification in the process. It was to be expected also that, as time passed, new stories would be produced and legendary elements would weave themselves among earlier, sounder parts of the tradition. It was also inevitable that as new meanings were found in ancient materials, the materials themselves would be altered to make these meanings more apparent. These developments we should expect to occur, and there can be no doubt that they did occur. When we deal, later in these lectures, with the way Jesus was interpreted in the early church, we shall have occasion to discuss at some length several examples of such modifications in the tradition. But some illustration of how this process worked may be valuable now. Let us look at the part of the tradition in which the process of change was under least control because there was little, if any, actual memory by which to check it — the tradition concerning Jesus' birth.

The earliest Gospel is the Gospel of Mark. Although it does not deal explicitly with the birth of Jesus, one would gather from it that Jesus was born in Nazareth of Galilee,[7] that his mother's name was Mary, and that she and several brothers and sisters of Jesus still lived there after Jesus' public career had begun. It is highly likely that this account in Mark represents a primitive memory, the more so as the Fourth Gospel also represents Jesus as coming from Nazareth. But it was soon noticed, in some communities at least, that according to the Scriptures the Messiah was to be born in Bethlehem of Judea. Since Jesus was the Messiah and since it was inconceivable that the Scriptures should be mistaken about his birthplace, this prediction became the most

---

[7] See Mark 1:9; 6:1. The use of the word πατρίς in Mark 6:1 is all but decisive. The word means " native city."

incontrovertible of evidence that Jesus had actually been born there.

Since no remembered fact threw any light upon why his parents were in Bethlehem when he was born (earlier tradition uniformly associating them with Nazareth), imagination was free to explain the circumstance in whatever seemed the most plausible way. We should not be surprised, therefore, to find that the two Gospels which tell us of Jesus' birth in Bethlehem offer quite different explanations: Matthew leaves us to understand that Joseph and Mary resided in Bethlehem when Jesus was born; that they remained there after his birth until just before Herod's murder of the infants, when they escaped to Egypt; that it was their intention to resume their residence in Bethlehem upon their return to Palestine, but fear of the new king of Judea led them to push on beyond their former home and to settle finally in Nazareth of Galilee. This is how it happened, as Matthew understands it, that one who had been born in Bethlehem came to be known as the Nazarene. Luke, on the other hand, understands that Mary and Joseph resided all the time in Nazareth; that they only chanced to be in Bethlehem when Jesus was born, having gone there for the purpose of being enrolled in a census; and that after Jesus' birth they returned to Nazareth again.

Even earlier than the Bethlehem tradition was the belief that Jesus was a descendant of David. This belief may, of course, have rested upon a genuine memory; but more probably it did not, since one passage, Mark 12:35 ff., attributes to Jesus himself a denial that the Messiah would be of Davidic descent and, implicitly, that he himself was.[8]

---

[8] This passage is as follows: "And Jesus answered and said while he taught in the temple, How do the scribes say that the Christ is the son of David? For David himself said by the Holy Spirit, The Lord said to my Lord, Sit thou on my right hand till I make thine enemies thy footstool. David therefore himself calleth him Lord; and whence is he his son?" This

Besides, such a belief would so naturally have developed in the church in the same way that belief in the Bethlehem birthplace developed: According to the Scriptures (the kind of exegesis represented by Mark 12:35 ff. proved too strained and tortuous), the Messiah was to be the son of David; but *Jesus* was the Messiah; therefore, he was the son of David.

But whether Jesus' descent from David was a genuine memory or an inference from his messiahship, the two quite different genealogies which in Matthew and Luke support this belief can hardly have belonged to the most primitive tradition. Both of them cannot be true, and it is doubtful that either is. They would have been produced during the period when Christians were supporting the claim of Davidic descent for Jesus against Jewish denials, and the discrepancies between them indicate the lack of any authentic or authoritative source of information.

Still another step may be noted in the growth of the birth-story tradition in the period in which the Synoptic Gospels were being compiled. Both genealogies presuppose that Jesus was born in the normal way and therefore trace the descent through Joseph. Later, however, it became widely believed that Jesus was born of the Virgin Mary. The two genealogies were too firmly established in the tradition to be discarded or corrected, although they are utterly incompat-

---

passage may represent an authentic conversation of Jesus, or it may have been developed out of the experiences of the later church. If authentic, it must mean that Jesus did not believe the Messiah would be or, at least, needed to be, a descendant of David. In that event, it is virtually impossible to suppose that the very early community which remembered and preserved this remark of Jesus and presumably used it in its preaching and teaching held a different view. More probably, however, the remark is not authentic. In that event, it can hardly have been developed except to refute those (probably Jewish) opponents who insisted that Jesus could not be the Messiah because he was not a descendant of David. As we shall see almost at once, the later answer to this charge was the claim that he *was* a son of David; apparently an earlier answer was that he did not need to be. But the claim to Davidic descent goes back quite early, as Rom. 1:3 indicates.

ible with the new belief. Both Gospel writers make super-
ficial changes in the genealogies, attempting to smooth out
the discrepancy, but actually they only call attention to it.
Matthew concludes his account with the words: " And Jacob
begat Joseph, the husband of Mary, of whom was born
Jesus, who is called Christ "; and Luke begins his: " And
Jesus was about thirty years of age, being (as was supposed)
the son of Joseph, which was the son of Heli . . ." Luke's
phrase, " as was supposed," betrays particularly clearly that
he is attempting to bring an old tradition into line with a
later belief with which it was originally and is still essentially incompatible. It may also be noted in this connection that the story of Jesus' birth in Bethlehem which Luke
adopts had apparently taken form before this belief
emerged. Why should it be assumed that Mary would ac-
company Joseph to Bethlehem unless they were man and
wife? Undoubtedly, when this story was first told, they
were represented as such. Luke brings the story into line
with the new conception by placing the word " affianced "
before " wife," but he cannot so easily destroy the sure
traces of an earlier and simpler view.

My reason for reviewing the birth stories in Matthew
and Luke is not that I regard them as typical of the extent of change the primitive memories of Jesus suffered
before the Gospels fixed the tradition in the form in which
we possess it. This part of the tradition underwent more
extensive and rapid change than any other simply because
interest in Jesus' birth developed relatively late and there
was no solid body of remembered fact by which to check the
growth of legend. We are not surprised that this growth
proceeded so swiftly that by the end of the second century
whole Gospels are devoted to stories of Jesus' birth and boyhood, all of them palpably without the slightest foundation. I have cited the tradition of Jesus' birth because the

very extensiveness and rapidity of its development enable us to see there more clearly than elsewhere the principles of change which were in some degree operative throughout the whole tradition. In every part of it original memory is mixed with later interpretation and is often modified by it; but one has only to compare the canonical Gospels with such later apocryphal Gospels as the Protevangelium of James or the Gospel of Thomas [9] to see that the body of remembered fact and impression was throughout the first century substantial enough to prevent the wild growth of the tradition.

Indeed, it is striking that the same critical tests which, when applied to the birth stories, reveal so large an element of legend, have the effect, rather, of establishing the validity of the Gospel record when they are applied to the main body of the tradition, the Synoptic account of Jesus' public career. One of the most prevalent misunderstandings of the meaning of historical criticism as applied to the Gospels has been the supposition that the method has had only negative results. The fact is that for every alleged fact discredited, another has been the more firmly established, and the increased confidence with which we can accept certain elements in the tradition more than compensates for doubts cast on other elements.

Consider, for example, the tradition concerning Jesus' early connection with John the Baptist. In Mark we are told simply that Jesus was baptized by John in the river Jordan. This was the primitive memory. But we can see that this baptism would cause growing embarrassment: Why should Jesus have been baptized by John — the greater by the less? And was not John's baptism a " baptism of re-

---

[9] These and other noncanonical Gospels are most readily available in Montague Rhodes James, *The Apocryphal New Testament* (London: Oxford University Press, 1924) .

pentance "? How then could he who was really the Christ have accepted it? The whole question of Jesus' baptism by John was the more important and disturbing because at the end of the first century disciples of the Baptist were challenging the primacy of Jesus over John and were doubtless appealing to the baptism as one of their principal arguments.[10] But the baptism was too well remembered to be denied, although the Fourth Gospel, written in the early second century, can be silent about it. Luke manages to avoid saying explicitly that John baptized Jesus, and in Matthew's Gospel Mark's simple account is amplified by the inclusion of a protest on the part of John against the impropriety of his baptizing Jesus when really Jesus should be baptizing him. In other words, John himself is made to state the Christian case against the followers of John. This is evidently a legendizing addition; but the remembered facts are clear enough. The very signs of the difficulty the early church had with the tradition at this point establish its validity. The baptism would never have been affirmed if it had not been remembered.

[10] The best summary known to me of the evidence for the existence and importance of a John the Baptist sect is to be found in an article in the *American Journal of Theology* (Jan. 1912) by Clayton R. Bowen, " John the Baptist in the New Testament." This article was later reprinted in a volume of Dr. Bowen's collected papers, edited by Robert J. Hutcheon and published under the title, *Studies in the New Testament* (Chicago: University of Chicago Press, 1936), pp. 49 ff. The following paragraph, quoted by permission of the University of Chicago Press, will be illuminating: " Justin Martyr, who began his Christian life in Ephesus, knows a sect of Jews called Baptists (*Trypho*, 80). Hegesippus, a little later, gives a similar list of Jewish sects, including ' Hemerobaptists ' (Eus. IV, xxii, 7). These Hemerobaptists meet us again in the Apostolic Constitutions, in Epiphanius, in the Talmud, and elsewhere. The Clementine Homilies (II:23) speak of John as a Hemerobaptist, making the definite connection between this sect and his movement. The Clementine Recognitions (I:60) has this passage: ' One of the disciples of John asserted that John was the Messiah, and not Jesus, inasmuch as Jesus himself declared that John was greater than all men and all prophets. If then, said he, he be greater than all, he must be held to be greater than Moses and than Jesus himself. But if he be the greatest of all, then he must be the Messiah.' "

The same kind of test confirms such facts as that the major part of Jesus' public career lay in Galilee rather than in Jerusalem and Judea, and that he was actually put to death by the Roman rather than by the Jewish authorities. In the later Gospels a strong tendency was at work to emphasize the importance of Jerusalem in Jesus' ministry. Once the church had become largely Gentile (and this happened very soon [11]), the tendency to associate Jesus with the most important center of Palestine — indeed, the only center of which the average Gentile would have heard perhaps — is understandable. That the association of Jesus with Galilee should have been invented is unthinkable; on the contrary, if the fact had not been distinctly remembered it would have dropped from sight (as it has almost done in the Fourth Gospel) under the pressure of the tendency to emphasize the capital city. In the same way, it is clear that as the church became more and more exclusively Gentile, there was the strongest inclination to play down the part which Pilate and the Romans had in the crucifixion and to place the blame on the Jews. This inclination, which reaches its extreme expression in some of the later apocryphal literature, clearly appears in the canonical narratives. But the fact that Jesus was crucified under Pontius Pilate could not be denied, however it might be mitigated, explained, or condoned. Again, we can be surer of the fact than before the critical tests were applied.

All of these items — Jesus' Nazareth origin, his baptism by John, the Galilean locale of his ministry, his execution by the Gentiles — are examples of facts of which we can be especially sure because later interests and beliefs of the churches would have led to a denial of them if they had not

[11] It is clear that by the time Paul wrote his letter to the Romans this had happened. In chaps. 9–11 Paul is dealing with the *fact* that the Jews have, by and large, rejected the gospel and the church has become an almost entirely Gentile community.

been well authenticated and firmly established. Other examples of this kind will appear in the course of this discussion. It would be arbitrary, however, to decide that nothing is to be trusted which does not pass this test. The fact that an item sustains a later belief or serves a later need does not mean *ipso facto* that it cannot be regarded as belonging to the earliest tradition. Only when it *also* fails to conform to the original situation as our most primitive sources give it to us is such an item suspect. The burden of proof falls on those who deny, not on those who affirm, the authenticity of any given item in the Gospel story. But I have said enough to show that in many instances that burden can be easily carried.

Although these lectures can attempt no full or detailed account of the life of Jesus, it is in order to state briefly what, so far as we can know, was the early church's understanding of the major formal facts of his career. As I have said and as we would have expected, little, if anything, was remembered about Jesus' birth and boyhood. It was known that he had come from Nazareth in Galilee, and in all probability it was assumed, or known, that he had been born there. He was the eldest in a family of several brothers and sisters, some of whom at least, whatever their attitude toward him may have been during his lifetime, were later prominent members of the community of believers. Paul speaks of the " brethren of the Lord " as being among the early evangelists and refers to " James, the Lord's brother," who was apparently the head of the Jerusalem church.[12] Jesus doubtless received an elementary education in the synagogue school at Nazareth. His father was a carpenter and there is no reason to doubt that Jesus learned that trade.

[12] I Cor. 9:5; Gal. 1:19.

There is every indication that he was brought up in a pious Jewish home of what we would call the economic and social lower middle class.

It was the preaching of John the Baptist which seems to have led immediately to Jesus' forsaking the quietness and obscurity of his Nazareth life and undertaking his public work. We have already seen how strong is the tradition associating the inauguration of his teaching career with this preacher of God's righteousness, this herald of God's approaching judgment, this voice calling Israel to repentance. About the character of Jesus' own message I shall speak later. While not failing to strike these same notes of righteousness, judgment, and repentance, it differed as widely from John's message as his manner of life differed from that of the austere prophet, who lived alone in the desert, was clothed in camel's hair, and " came neither eating nor drinking." Jesus taught and healed in the villages and towns of Galilee, surrounded by multitudes and, more intimately, by a little group of disciples, mostly fishermen and artisans, who accompanied him on his journeys through the countryside and to and fro across the lake of Galilee. Capernaum, a city on the lake, appears to have been his most frequent place of residence.

There is no way of knowing how long his public work continued. Since only one Passover is mentioned in the Synoptic Gospels, it is likely that his active career was a matter of months or, at most, a year. As the Passover approached, he determined to go to Jerusalem, although growing opposition to him among the leaders of official Judaism warned him of danger there.[13] This danger

---

13 Although there can be no doubt, as we have seen, that Jesus was put to death by the Roman authorities, I cannot agree with those who virtually deny any hostility toward him on the part of the authorized religious leaders of the people, especially the Pharisees. The actual death of Jesus was perpetrated by the Romans (indeed, the use of crucifixion would

quickly materialized.   Perhaps it was the enthusiasm of
Galilean pilgrims, who hailed him as Messiah as he entered
the city, which called Jesus to the unfavorable notice of the
Roman authorities; perhaps it was Jesus' own act of driv-
ing money-changers from the temple courts; perhaps it was
the bringing of charges against him by powerful Jewish
groups whom he had offended.   We cannot know just how
it happened, but the Roman government was led to see in
him a possible revolutionary.   He was secretly arrested,
summarily tried, and quickly executed.

   Such, very briefly, are the major formal facts of Jesus'
career.   One cannot state them without realizing afresh
how unilluminating and really unimportant such facts
often are.   Statistics are rarely vital.   In this case they do
not give us the slightest hint that the life to which they re-
late was the greatest life ever lived and marked the most important moment in the long history of mankind.   For the
secret of both that greatness and that importance one must
look, not to the public facts about his life, but to what he
actually meant to the few who knew and loved him.   The
clue to understanding the whole historical significance of
Jesus lies in the meaning of Jesus in the early church.

---

itself indicate this) , perhaps with the assistance, if not at the instigation, of
some of the priestly hierarchy at Jerusalem, who probably feared a " dis-
turbance " even more than the Roman officers did.   But there is every reason to believe that before the rapidly climactic events of the final week
began, Jesus had offended the official leaders, Pharisees as well as Sad-
ducees.   This hostility, according to the highly credible account in Mark
2:1–3:6, grew out of the threat Jesus constituted to the authority of the
" law " as it was conventionally interpreted and to the authority of its
trained and duly ordained interpreters.   His teaching and practice threat-
ened the mores, the ways of life, to which official Judaism attached much
more importance than to formal beliefs merely as such.   His way of conceiving God's righteous will was nothing short of revolutionary, and the
opposition of vested interests, religious as well as political, should not be
surprising.

Lecture II

JESUS was remembered as a teacher and prophet, and not only the more important emphases of his teaching but also many of his actual words were remembered. For this memory, especially of his words, we are largely dependent upon Matthew and Luke, but these writers are obviously drawing upon earlier sources. Mark does not give us any extensive account of the content of Jesus' discourses, but often refers to him as a prophet and a teacher. And although Paul, earlier still, does not call him by either name, some knowledge of him as a teacher or prophet must be presupposed in the references to the " words of the Lord," which have for Paul such pre-eminent authority.

The burden of Jesus' preaching seems to have been the proclamation of the kingdom of God. Mark tells us that Jesus began his public career with the announcement: " The kingdom of God is at hand; repent and believe the gospel "; [1] and all the accounts of his teaching in the Synoptic Gospels are so filled with the phrase that we cannot question its importance for Jesus — the more so as the infrequency of its appearance in the Epistles would indicate that it was not used especially often in the early church.

But constantly as Jesus apparently used the words " kingdom of God," we are not too sure of what he meant by them. Here is one of the most intricate problems in New Testament study; and although in these lectures we cannot attempt a thorough treatment of Jesus' teaching any more than of his life, nevertheless we cannot avoid giving some at-

[1] Mark 1:14-15.

23

tention to this problem. This is true not only because of
its intrinsic importance, but also because it is involved in
the question of how Jesus came to be interpreted in the
early church, a matter with which we shall later be concerned.

The difficulty of deciding just what Jesus' first hearers
understood him to be saying about the kingdom of God
grows out of the ambiguity of the Aramaic phrase rendered
in Greek by the words, ἡ Βασιλεία τοῦ Θεοῦ. No single
English phrase conveys the full and varied significance of
the term. Three meanings can be distinguished, although
none of the three is really complete when it is separated
from the others: (1) the eternal, ultimate sovereignty of
God, his kingship (as in the familiar, " Thine is the kingdom and the power and the glory forever and ever ") ;
(2) the rule of God in and among men in so far as God's
sovereignty is acknowledged and his will is done; (3) the
complete and perfect establishment of God's rule in the
" age to come." In the first sense, the kingdom was real —
indeed, the ultimate reality — but was not yet actual; in
the second sense, it was actual but imperfect and incom-
plete; in the third sense, it would be both actual and complete. In the first sense, one would *acknowledge* the kingdom of God; in the second sense, one might belong to it
even now; in the third sense, one would expect and hope
for it. In the first sense, the kingdom was above history;
in the second, it was within history; in the third, it was at
the end, or beyond the end, of history. Once it is seen that
the same phrase might be used in all or any of these closely
related but distinguishable senses, there will be no surprise
that contemporary students of the Gospels differ in their
understanding of what Jesus meant.

The dimensions of the problem can, perhaps, be indicated most clearly if we consider the three views which

settle on one or another of the three possible meanings of the term as being its normative meaning for Jesus. Those who hold these views, without denying the ambiguity of the phrase "kingdom of God," nevertheless affirm that Jesus was more or less consistent and specific in his use of it; but they disagree as to just which of the three possible, or partial, meanings of the term Jesus had primarily in mind.

There are, first, the "consistent eschatologists," of whom Albert Schweitzer is the best known representative.[2] These interpreters take the third meaning as normative and assert not only that Jesus expected the imminent and catastrophic end of history and the present world and God's establishment of a new order in which his righteous purpose would be perfectly fulfilled, but also that whenever he spoke of the "kingdom of God" he used the phrase in that sense and in that sense only. The strenuous and absolute character of Jesus' ethic is explained as owing to his belief in the imminence of the great catastrophe: it was an "interim ethic."

At the opposite extreme from Schweitzer and his school are those liberal interpreters who regard the second sense of the "kingdom of God" as normative for Jesus. According to these interpreters, the passages in the teaching of Jesus which suggest that he expected the early end of history have been read back into his words by the later church,

---

[2] The important works of Schweitzer dealing with this subject are *Das Messianitäts und Leidensgeheimnis: Eine Skizze des Lebens Jesu* (Tübingen, 1901), English translation by W. Lowrie, *The Mystery of the Kingdom of God* (New York: Dodd, Mead & Co., 1914); and *Von Reimarus zu Wrede: Eine Geschichte der Leben-Jesu-Forschung* (Tübingen, 1906), English translation by W. Montgomery, *The Quest of the Historical Jesus* (London: A. & C. Black, 1910). Schweitzer's earlier work was antedated by the significant study of Johannes Weiss, *Die Predigt Jesu vom Reiche Gottes* (Göttingen, 1892). For recent interpretations of reactions to Schweitzer's position see A. Wilder, *Eschatology and Ethics in the Teaching of Jesus* (New York: Harper & Brothers, 1939), pp. 28 ff., and C. C. McCown, *The Search for the Real Jesus* (New York: Charles Scribner's Sons, 1940), pp. 238 ff.

itself immersed in apocalyptic hopes and speculations.
Jesus meant by the " kingdom of God " simply the rule of
God in so far as it was and could be realized by men living
under the normal conditions of human life. Those who
acknowledge his kingship and seek to do his will already belong to his " kingdom "; and this, according to this understanding, is the only meaning the term has in Jesus' authentic teaching. This view is historically the least tenable of
the three consistent views, but, because it is the most congenial to our modern mood, is probably held by the largest
number of modern readers. H. B. Sharman may be mentioned as one of the few serious defenders of this interpretation.[3]

The third possible consistent position is defended by
C. H. Dodd and has had in the last decade a very great influence. Dodd holds, in effect, that Jesus used the phrase
" kingdom of God " chiefly in the first sense — the eternal
righteous sovereignty of God — but that he believed this
" kingdom " was being manifested in a unique and supreme way in his own life and works.[4] Jesus was not an-

[3] See Sharman, *The Teaching of Jesus About the Future* (Chicago: University of Chicago Press, 1909) and *Son of Man and Kingdom of God* (New
York: Harper & Brothers, 1943).

[4] Dodd has used the term " realized eschatology " to designate his position (set forth most clearly in *The Parables of the Kingdom* [New York:
Charles Scribner's Sons, 1935]) and in so doing conceals somewhat, it seems
to me, its essential character. The phrase " realized eschatology " suggests
that the end of history has now come. This, as we shall see, is Rudolf
Otto's understanding of Jesus' thought (see below, pp. 28 f.) and, therefore,
the phrase might well be used to describe Otto's view, the participle being
taken as a present: " eschatology being realized." But I submit that Dodd's
position, although it is not independent of Otto's, is essentially different.
Dodd does not believe that Jesus thought of the kingdom as *coming* at all,
either now or later, if by " coming " we mean either actually becoming historical or (so to speak) displacing history. It is a suprahistorical reality
which has " come " in Jesus only in the sense that it is supremely present,
active and potent in him. It is now " revealed " — it being understood, of
course, that by " revelation " is meant an actual presence and activity (see
below, pp. 68 ff.), not a mere announcement or declaration. This view
is stated most clearly and unequivocally on pp. 107 f. of Dodd's book, just

nouncing a future event or referring to a future order when
he spoke of the kingdom; he was referring to an eternal
Reality which, nevertheless, was then and there making
itself known — that is, was present and active within history — in a way both unprecedented and unduplicable.
Dodd relies greatly on Jesus' assertion: "The kingdom of
God has come upon you."[5] He interprets this to mean:
"In me, in my words and deeds, the sovereign power of
God confronts you. You are now judged. God's salvation
is now offered you." In no other sense than this would the
kingdom of God ever "come."

Perhaps these three "consistent" views can be more
clearly distinguished if we ask what was Jesus' conception
of the *time* of the kingdom's coming. Schweitzer would
say it was a future event, but so imminent that Jesus could
sometimes speak of it as though it had already occurred.
Sharman would reply that the kingdom for Jesus was past,
present and future — future only in the sense in which it
was also present and past. Dodd would answer that the
kingdom was neither past nor future, nor yet present. It
was an eternal reality — above and beyond time altogether
— although it was revealed in time and active in time, supremely in Jesus' own life and work.

It is not necessary to choose among these three views.
There is no reason to assume that Jesus' use of the phrase
"kingdom of God" was simple or consistent. He doubtless
employed the phrase in all three of the senses we have been
discussing. That Jesus was aware with every breath he
drew of the eternal kingship of God everyone will agree;
that he believed men could come even now in some real
sense and measure under the righteous and loving rule of

cited. See also the excellent criticism of Dodd's position by C. T. Craig,
"Realized Eschatology," *Journal of Biblical Literature,* LVI (March 1937),
pp. 17 ff.
    5 Matt. 12:28; Luke 11:20.

God is almost equally clear; and only by the most tortuous methods of interpreting the Gospels can one escape the conclusion that Jesus expected the kingdom of God as a future supernatural order.

If the phrase had all three meanings for him, it is likely that whenever he used it all three meanings were in some measure present in his mind. The eternal kingship of God implied for him the eventual vindication of God's righteousness in the end or beyond the end of history, and implied meantime the possibility of man's accepting and submitting himself to God's rule. We may assume that none of these closely related meanings was ever entirely absent from his thought when he spoke of the kingdom, but one of them might on any given occasion be primary. It is not unlikely that the eschatological meaning was frequently dominant. Nor do I believe we can accept Dodd's view that Jesus thought of the whole meaning of the eschatological hope of Israel as being exhausted in the manifestation of the will and power of God which was taking place in and through his own person. It may well be true that the whole meaning of eschatology is *for us* fulfilled in the revelation in Christ — that is, in the active presence in Christ as known within the church — of the eternal order, the kingdom of God: the Fourth Gospel has some such conception. But it is impossible to ascribe such a view to Jesus without doing too much violence to the tradition. Jesus expected the fulfillment in a future — although immediately future — order.

It is necessary to allude to one other modern interpretation of Jesus' teaching about the kingdom, that of Rudolf Otto.[6] Otto argues that although in Jesus' thought the

⁶ See *Reichgottes und Menschensohn* (München, 1934), English translation by F. V. Filson and B. L. Woolf, *The Kingdom of God and the Son of Man* (London and Grand Rapids, Mich.: Zondervan Publishing House, 1938-39).

kingdom was always primarily eschatological, it was nevertheless a present fact. It could be both eschatological and present simply because the final eschatological events had already begun to occur. In Jesus' own life, in his words and acts, the supernatural kingdom was beginning; the consummation was still to come, but the final crisis of history had already broken. It is thus that Otto interprets the passage already referred to: "The kingdom of God has come upon you."

To me it seems not unlikely that Jesus did think of the kingdom in some such way: as already being realized. Much in the Gospels suggests that Jesus thought of himself not merely as announcing the crisis of history but as being himself a factor in the crisis. Certainly the first Christian generation so interpreted him. For these first believers the final crisis was not merely to come; it had come. Their eschatology was both present and future. They were themselves in the midst of the final judging, saving act of God. The career of Jesus was the beginning of a mighty eschatological event with which history was rapidly coming to an end. This understanding of the significance of the moment in which they stood and of the relation of Jesus to it may well go back to a primitive memory of how Jesus himself understood the significance of the events of which he was the center.

I rejected a moment ago Dodd's view that for Jesus the whole meaning of eschatology was fulfilled in the revelation of the sovereign righteousness of God which was taking place in him; I find it impossible to deny the element of the temporal in Jesus' thought about the judgment and the kingdom. But this part of our discussion may appropriately end with the remark that, although this is true, nevertheless the expectation of a future crisis need not represent the whole of Jesus' meaning when he says that the kingdom

of God, even in some absolute sense, is at hand. There are
other kinds of immediacy besides temporal immediacy; and
Dodd has rendered a great service in making us more vividly aware of that fact. Indeed, I do not believe one is distorting or modernizing the teaching of Jesus when one
denies that even for him the whole meaning of the immediacy of the kingdom was exhausted by the expected future
crisis. The kingdom of God could be thought of as imminent in the future only because in another sense it is constantly present. It *will* come soon because it *is* near. The
kingdom, in this absolute sense, did not come soon — it did
not come at all — but it is still near. We are each moment
under the awful judgment of God and the forgiveness of
God is being in each moment freely offered us. Thus in its
deepest sense — may we not say, even for Jesus? — the text
is still true: " The time *is* fulfilled; the kingdom of God *is*
at hand." The time is always being fulfilled; the kingdom
of God is always at hand; not as a future event perhaps, but
in the profounder sense of an ever present reality, both
within our life and above it, both immanent and transcend-
ent.

Because we shall later be specifically concerned with the
way Jesus was understood and interpreted in the early
church, we cannot avoid paying some attention to another
difficult problem — the problem of how Jesus thought of
the relation in which he himself stood toward the eschatological kingdom of God. Was he merely the prophet, the
herald, of the coming judgment and salvation, or did he
stand in some closer and more important relation to it? I
have just indicated, in referring to Rudolf Otto's views,
that there are many passages in the Gospels which suggest
that Jesus thought of himself as being not simply an an-

nouncer of a future event but also an actor or participant
in an event already beginning to occur. Just how did he
think of his own role? No question about Jesus can be
asked with less likelihood of an assured answer, but the
question must be asked nevertheless if we would approach
an understanding of the meaning of Jesus in the early
church.

There were current in the circles in which Jesus lived
at least four or five ways of thinking of the agency through
which God would judge the world and inaugurate the age
to come. Of these, three were apparently more widely
prevalent than others. According to one view, there would
be no agent at all: God would directly, without any inter-
mediary, set up his kingdom and would himself reign.
This view we may call the " theocratic " conception of the
kingdom. A second conception was " messianic " — God
would act through an anointed king, a descendant of David,
to defeat his enemies and establish his kingdom. This
" Messiah " (or his dynasty) would either reign forever or
else would reign for a certain time, perhaps a thousand
years, and then would surrender the rule to God, when the
" millennial " kingdom of the Messiah would become the
everlasting kingdom of God. The third conception was
that of the " Son of Man " — a heavenly being of human aspect who, according to some of the apocalypses, would appear in glory to judge the world.[7] In this conception, the
inauguration of the new age would be an entirely supernatural process and God's agent would be an altogether
supernatural figure. There is no sufficient evidence that
before Jesus' time the " Messiah " and " Son of Man "

[7] In Dan. 7:13 f. there is an account of the appearance in the apocalyptic
vision of one " like unto a son of man." This being clearly symbolizes Israel
and follows the appearance of several beasts, which represent various for-
eign powers. In Enoch 37–71 and in II Esdras 13, this being has been
personalized and has assumed some of the functions of the Messiah.

conceptions had been fused, although — within Christianity, at any rate — that development eventually took place.
The two titles represented two different ways of conceiving
God's agent or vicegerent in the final crisis.

Which of these conceptions did Jesus hold, or did he
hold any of them? We can answer with some assurance that
he did not expect a " Messiah " in the strict, somewhat political sense in which that term has just been defined. The
kingdom of God was for Jesus not a resurgent Israel under
a victorious Davidic king — even an Israel generous toward her erstwhile enemies and persecutors, as in Jeremiah and parts of Isaiah. Some of Jesus' disciples may
have held such a view, but everything indicates that Jesus
did not. It is possible that his thinking about the kingdom
was simply theocratic, and many competent modern interpreters claim that this was the case; [8] but this would mean
that all the references in the Synoptic Gospels to the eschatological Son of Man have been read into Jesus' teaching by the early church.

We are certainly safe in saying that Jesus thought of the
" fulfillment of all things " either in theocratic or in apocalyptic " Son of Man " terms. The decision between these
two possibilities is complicated by the fact that whereas
there can be little question that Jesus used the phrase " son
of man," [9] it is again (as in the case of the " kingdom of

[8] Among these may be mentioned S. J. Case, *Jesus: A New Biography*
(Chicago: University of Chicago Press, 1927) , and F. C. Grant, *The Gospel
of the Kingdom* (New York: Macmillan Co., 1940) .

[9] The ground for this assurance is not merely the Gospel testimony that
Jesus used the phrase; it is rather that it appears so often on his lips and
nowhere else. In the Synoptic Gospels Jesus is said to have spoken of the
Son of Man no fewer than 69 times (38 times when parallel passages are
disregarded) , but the evangelists themselves make no use of the term. The
same thing is true of the Fourth Gospel with one or two possible exceptions.
Acts 7:56 is the only clear exception to this rule in the New Testament
and contains the only use of the phrase as applied to Jesus outside of
the Gospels. Apparently the early churches generally did not use the
term, but there was a clear memory that Jesus had used it. On this whole

God ") not clear in what sense he used it, for the Aramaic word of which " son of man " is the literal translation was an ambiguous term.

The phrase " son of man," whether in Hebrew or Aramaic, might apparently be used to mean simply " man " or " a man." [10] An illustration of this generic use appears in the parallelism of the Psalm:

> What is man that thou art mindful of him?
> And the son of man that thou visitest him? [11]

And the individual sense is exemplified in the words, " O son of man," with which Ezekiel is addressed. There seems little reason to doubt that Jesus may have used the phrase in this common sense.

But the term had also come to be widely employed, as we have seen, to refer to the heavenly person who would be manifest in the last days, and in many of its occurrences on Jesus' lips it has this meaning. For example, consider the following passages selected almost at random from the several Synoptic Gospels:

For the son of man shall come in the glory of his father with his angels; and then shall he reward every man according to his deeds. Verily I say unto you, there are some standing here who shall not taste of death till they see the son of man coming in his kingdom. (Matt. 16:27 f. Cf. Mark 8:38–9:1; Luke 9:26 f.)

---

matter see F. J. Foakes-Jackson and K. Lake, *Beginnings of Christianity* (Part I, Vol. I. London: Macmillan Co., 1920), pp. 345 ff. (especially 374 ff.).

[10] That this is true in Hebrew no one denies. G. Dalman questions that it was true in Aramaic (*The Words of Jesus* [Edinburgh: T. & T. Clark, 1902], pp. 234 ff.), but there are many to differ from him. Cf., e.g., Joseph Klausner, *Jesus of Nazareth* (New York: Macmillan Co., 1925), pp. 256 f. For a full discussion see H. Lietzmann, *Der Menschensohn* (Freiburg and Leipzig, 1896).

[11] Ps. 8:4. Other instances of this usage, whether generic or individual, are: Job 25:6; 35:8; Pss. 144:3; 146:3; Isa. 51:12; 56:2; Jer. 49:18; 51:43; Dan. 8:17.

But when they persecute you in this city, flee to another; for verily I say unto you, Ye shall not have gone through the cities of Israel, till the son of man come. (Matt. 10:23)

In the regeneration, when the son of man shall sit on the throne of his glory. . . . (Matt. 19:28)

Watch ye therefore, and pray always that ye may be accounted worthy to escape all these things that shall come to pass and to stand before the son of man. (Luke 21:36)

For as the lightning cometh forth from the east and shineth even unto the west, so shall be the coming of the son of man. (Matt. 24:27; Luke 17:24)

And then shall they see the son of man coming in clouds of heaven with power and great glory. (Matt. 24:30; Mark 13:26; Luke 21:27)

Therefore be ye also ready: for in such an hour as ye think not the son of man cometh. (Matt. 24:44; cf. Matt. 25:13)

When the son of man shall come in his glory and all the holy angels with him, then shall he sit upon the throne of his glory. (Matt. 25:31)

And ye shall see the son of man sitting on the right hand of power and coming on the clouds of heaven. (Mark 14:62; Matt. 26:64)

The eschatological significance of the phrase " son of man " in such passages cannot be denied, but many deny the authenticity of the passages themselves. These interpreters hold that Jesus used the phrase only in its ordinary sense of " man," and that some community in which the Gospel tradition was being formed, itself thinking of Jesus as the apocalyptic Son of Man, read that meaning back into Jesus' words. This is possible; but the fact that no early community can be found which felt any special interest in the title " Son of Man " makes it hardly probable. Paul, for example, does not use it,[12] and even in Mark and the

---

[12] Something will be said later about Paul's conception of Christ as " the second man from heaven " (I Cor. 15:47 ff.). It is enough at the moment to say that the whole context of this remark of Paul makes unlikely that he has in mind the Son of Man of Daniel or Enoch. But see C. H. Kraeling, *Anthropos and Son of Man* (New York: Columbia University Press, 1927), especially pp. 174 ff.

other Synoptics, as we have already observed, it is only
Jesus who uses the title; the Gospel writers themselves
never use it, nor does any other person in their narratives.
There would appear to be a genuine memory that Jesus not
only used the title but that he used it in an eschatological
sense.

This would not mean that he employed it only in that
sense. He probably used the title with both meanings —
that is, to designate both man and the Son of Man — but
because the eschatological seemed the more important to
the early church (especially since it was soon believed that
Jesus was alluding to himself when he used the term), it
was inevitable that all of Jesus' uses of the phrase should be
interpreted in that sense and, if necessary, conformed to it.
Thus an original statement of Jesus that the Sabbath was
made for man and that the " son of man " (that is, man) is
master of the Sabbath becomes an affirmation that the Son
of Man (that is, Jesus himself as God's vicegerent) is Lord
of the Sabbath.[13] There were no doubt many cases of this
kind — most of them no longer identifiable in the Gospels.[14]

I have just alluded to the impression established in the
early church, certainly as early as the Gospel of Mark, that
Jesus was speaking of himself when he referred to the eschatological Son of Man. Can we trust that impression as
going back to Jesus' first hearers and associates? There can
be no question that the Gospels represent him as thinking
of himself in this way, just as they also represent him as

[13] Cf. Mark 2:27 f. with Matt. 12:8 and Luke 6:5. This is a particularly
illuminating case. Mark reads: " The Sabbath was made for man and
not man for the Sabbath: therefore the son of man is lord also of the Sabbath." It is clear that even for Mark the " son of man " is Jesus, not mankind. Matthew and Luke regard this part of Jesus' statement, thus understood, as being so incomparably the important part of it that they merely
omit the priceless " The Sabbath was made for man and not man for the
Sabbath."

[14] Is it possible that Mark 2:10 (Matt. 9;6; Luke 5:24) and Matt. 12:32
(Luke 12:10) are other instances?

regarding himself as the Messiah.[15]   But several considera-
tions will put us on guard against accepting these repre-
sentations too quickly.

The first of these is the obvious fact that once the early
church came to think of Jesus as being a heavenly eschatological Redeemer (whether it used the title " Son of Man "
or not) it was inevitable that it should regard him as having
thought of himself in that same way, even if nothing in the
remembered tradition of his words gave specific support
to that view.   But if Jesus actually often used the phrase
" son of man " (as he almost certainly did), and especially
if he used it, even occasionally, in the apocalyptic sense (as
he probably did), the tradition would have seemed to offer
the strongest support to the view.   Since Jesus *was* the Messiah and since " son of man " was in some circles a recognized messianic title, obviously (it would seem to the early
churches) he was referring to himself when he spoke of the
Son of Man.   It would not have been necessary to read the
words " son of man " into the tradition; that phrase was already there.   Only the slightest changes would have been
required to bring the remembered teaching of Jesus about
the Son of Man into line with the faith that he was himself
the Son of Man.   These changes would have been made

[15] The case for Jesus' conscious messiahship, however, is considerably
less strong.   The term " messiah " or " king " occurs on Jesus' own lips
in the Synoptic Gospels only 13 times (39 times elsewhere), whereas, as
we have seen, " son of man " is found 69 times (and not once elsewhere).
A study of Mark 8:27–30; 14:61 f.; and 15:2–5, and parallels, will reveal
how very weak is the evidence that Jesus actually acknowledged the messiahship.   To be sure, he is not said to have denied it, but it is inconceivable that the early church could have accepted such a denial even if it
had been remembered.   There are only two accounts of Jesus' explicitly
accepting the title, Mark 14:62 and Matt. 16:17 ff.   More often Jesus is
silent or evasive when the question of messiahship is raised.   Matt. 16:17 ff.
appears very much like an insertion into the traditional story of Peter's confession.   Neither Mark nor Luke records any acknowledgment by Jesus
of the title of Messiah, which Peter has conferred.

quite unintentionally and unconsciously — or, if consciously, they would have been made with the purpose not
of distorting the tradition but of correcting and clarify-
ing it.

That this may well have happened is rendered more
probable by another consideration. Some students of Aramaic give us reason to believe that the term under discussion might be used to designate a particular man and that
it might sometimes have the meaning of " this man " —
that is, " I " or " me."[16]   Thus, Jesus may quite possibly
have used the phrase in speaking of himself, the so-called
messianic consciousness not being involved at all.   One of
the most likely instances of this is Jesus' warning to an over-
eager disciple that whereas the birds have nests and the
foxes have holes, the " son of man " does not have a place
to lay his head; the meaning may well be, if these linguists
are correct, " this man." [17]   If, now, Jesus not only used the
words " son of man " in speaking of the imminent end of
the age but also used them (in another sense) in speaking
of himself, the belief that he knew himself to be the eschatological Son of Man was certain to develop, once the church,
or any significant part of it, came to think of him as the
apocalyptic Judge and Savior.   Indeed, his having so
spoken of the Son of Man and of himself would virtually
assure that the early church *would* think of him in that way.

The probability that the primitive church, rather than
Jesus himself, is responsible for the identification of him
with the Son of Man is further confirmed by the fact that
the " Son of Man " passages in which this identification is

---

[16] See, for example, J. Héring, *Le Royaume de Dieu et sa venue* (Paris,
1937) , p. 104; see also Lietzmann, *op. cit.,* pp. 82 ff.   The present writer can
claim no competence in this field.

[17] Matt. 8:20; Luke 9:58. Is Matt. 11:18 f. (Luke 7:33 f.) another possible instance of this?

most explicit are, on the whole, not the eschatological passages. Where the words "son of man" are being most clearly used to designate the coming heavenly Judge, there is least evidence of self-identification.[18] Such evidence is strongest in those passages where Jesus is clearly referring to his own death, as in the following:

And he began to teach them that the son of man must suffer many things and be rejected by the elders and the chief priests and scribes, and be killed.   (Mark 8:31; Luke 9:22)

The son of man is delivered into the hands of men, and they shall kill him.   (Mark 9:31; Matt. 17:22; Luke 9:44)

Behold we go up to Jerusalem; and the son of man shall be delivered unto the chief priests and unto the scribes; and they shall condemn him to death, and shall deliver him to the Gentiles.   (Mark 10:33 f.; Matt. 20:18 f.; Luke 18:31 ff.)

The son of man came not to be ministered unto, but to minister, and to give his life a ransom for many.   (Mark 10:45)

In these passages, granted their authenticity, Jesus is plainly referring to himself, but he may be using the term "son of man" to mean "this man" or "I"; or he may have said "I" and the more impressive title was later substituted.   (It can be easily shown that this often happened, whether in these instances or not.)   It is noteworthy also, as Héring points out, that although many of the "Son of Man" passages refer to his own passion and many to the coming of the heavenly being on the clouds, none of them refers to both events together.[19]   This is not surprising: the idea that the apocalyptic Son of Man should die (and even before he had come!) would have been very difficult, if not

[18] Notice, for example, the passages cited on pp. 33 f.   In none of these does Jesus identify himself as the Son of Man, and in some cases it is exceedingly hard to harmonize Jesus' statement with such a belief on his part, as when he says, "When they persecute you in one city, flee to the next; for verily I say unto you, Ye shall not have gone through the cities of Israel till the Son of Man come"; or, "Be ye ready, for in such an hour as ye think not the Son of Man cometh."

[19] *Op. cit.*, p. 101.

impossible, to entertain, even if Isaiah 53 was taken " messianically," as was probably not the case so early.[20]

But the principal difficulty in the way of believing that Jesus thought of himself as the eschatological Son of Man is the psychological one. That one might come to regard oneself as Messiah is conceivable; indeed, it is known that many did so regard themselves and were so regarded by others. But the supernatural Son of Man conception seems far less possible of acceptance, either for oneself or by others. Rudolf Otto makes the most successful attempt to demonstrate that it was pyschologically possible for Jesus, in all sanity, to think of himself as actually being the future Son of Man. He bases his attempt upon the prevalence in Persia and more or less throughout the East of a type of thought which affirmed the existence in heaven of spiritual or angelic counterparts of persons living on the earth. According to Otto, Jesus thought of the heavenly Son of Man as thus corresponding to, in a real sense identical with, himself. Strong support, Otto holds, is lent this hypothesis by the Similitudes of Enoch (chapters 37–71) , which Charles

[20] Isaiah 53 is, of course, the principal passage of several in Isaiah dealing with the Servant of Yahweh, who was led " as a lamb to the slaughter," who bore the iniquities of others and by whose stripes others were healed. The early church found in these passages a clear and certain prophecy of the vicarious suffering of the Christ. There is no evidence, however, that the passage was understood by Jewish readers otherwise than as a reference to the nation of Israel, and this was surely the reference the prophet himself intended to make. Many Christian scholars hold that Jesus interpreted his role (and the meaning of messiahship) in terms of the Suffering Servant pattern. To me there seems too little evidence to support such a view. Indeed, the only passages which can be even claimed to do so are Mark 9:12, Mark 10:45 (quoted just above) , and Luke 22:37, although the many passages in which Jesus is represented as predicting that the Son of Man must die might be cited in partial support. According to this view, Jesus was original not only in taking the Suffering Servant as a type of the Messiah but also in combining this conception with that of the supernatural Son of Man. We are dealing with a matter far too difficult and perplexing to permit of one's dismissing easily and surely any possible interpretation, especially one held by so many serious and competent interpreters, but to me this view seems unlikely.

dates in the first century B.C. According to this document, Enoch, after many visions of heaven in which the Son of Man has appeared, is himself finally transported there. He is carried into higher and higher regions of heaven, undergoing various transformations, till finally he is brought into God's own presence. But nowhere has he seen the Son of Man, who had figured so prominently in his visions. According to Otto's interpretation of a disputed text, as Enoch wonders what this absence means, God says to him: " Thou art the Son of Man." Otto writes:

Long before Christ's appearance, a certain idea was fully developed in circles which had plainly formed long before him and to which he himself plainly belonged. The idea was that a powerful preacher alike of righteousness, the coming judgment, and the blessed new age, a prophet of the eschatological Son of Man, would be transported at the end of his earthly career to God; that he would be exalted to become the one whom he had proclaimed in the literal sense that he himself would become the very one he had proclaimed. But that also meant that his activity even during his earthly life was nothing else than the proleptic activity of this very redeemer.[21]

Otto's argument is impressive, and this summary, even including the quotation, does not do justice to it. But it falls short of being convincing. There is a vast difference between believing that an ancient worthy like Enoch (who walked with God and did not see death) became the Son of Man and believing that one will oneself become the Son of Man. Although Otto's suggestion may possibly throw light upon how the early church could have come to think of Jesus as being the Son of Man, it is a less promising clue to the understanding of how Jesus himself could have come to hold such a view.

The truth is that whereas after the resurrection it is not

[21] *The Kingdom of God and the Son of Man*, pp. 212 f. Quoted by permission of the Zondervan Publishing House.

difficult to understand the belief that Jesus was the heavenly Son of Man, it is hard to understand it before that event. This Son of Man is essentially a heavenly being: how could Jesus have been identified as such until he had become a heavenly being? I find it most reasonable to conclude that Jesus sometimes alluded to the coming of the Son of Man, that he may occasionally have referred to himself as a son of man or this son of man, and that the primitive church did the rest.

But the matter cannot be permitted to end just there. Although it seems to me unlikely that Jesus could have thought of himself as actually being the heavenly Son of Man, it does seem clear that he regarded himself as sustaining a connection of peculiar responsibility with the coming Judgment and as standing in some close relation with the advent of the Son of Man. God has intrusted to him some unique and supremely significant mission.[22] As to just how Jesus conceived of it we cannot know, if indeed his sense of divine vocation followed the lines of any particular conception. Héring, to whom I have been indebted at several points in this discussion, concludes his study of the appearances in the Synoptic Gospels of the phrase " Son of Man " in the eschatological sense with these three propositions:

[22] For example, Jesus is represented as saying, " For whosoever shall be ashamed of me and of my words in this adulterous and sinful generation, of him the Son of Man also will be ashamed, when he cometh in the glory of his Father with the holy angels " (Mark 8:38). This is reproduced almost verbatim in Luke 9:26. In Luke 12:8 f. we read this word of Jesus: " Whosoever shall confess me before men, him shall the Son of Man also confess before the angels of God; but he that denieth me before men shall be denied before the angels of God." Notice that in this passage Jesus is not represented as identifying himself with the Son of Man, although there is an intimate connection: men's attitude toward Jesus determines the attitude of the Son of Man toward them. In Matt. 10:32 f. the passage reads: " Whosoever therefore shall confess me before men, him will I also confess before my father which is in heaven. But whosoever shall deny me before men, him will I also deny before my father." Here, although Jesus is represented as thinking of himself as doing the " confessing," he does not speak of himself as the Son of Man.

1. Jesus professed faith in the coming of the Son of Man.

2. He indicates the existence of a soteriological connection between his earthly mission and the coming of the Son of Man; the attitude which men take toward the gospel will be the principle of judgment by the Son of Man.

3. He was in a mysterious way aware of a future identity between his own person and that of the Son of Man.[23]

The first two of these conclusions seem to me to be clearly indicated. I am not so sure of the third, but would prefer it to a denial of any uniqueness in Jesus' consciousness of his own relation to the imminent redemption. The ascription of messianic honors to Jesus by the early church, although it does not need to be so explained, and cannot in any case be adequately so explained, can nevertheless be more easily explained, if it was remembered that Jesus gave evidence of knowing himself to be in some unique and mysterious way related to the coming crisis of judgment and salvation.[24]

---

[23] *Le Royaume de Dieu et sa venue,* pp. 95 f.

[24] If the term "Messiah" could have been taken in the general sense of "one appointed of God" to the task of proclaiming "the nearness of the Realm of God and also its true character," as B. H. Branscomb suggests in his *The Gospel of Mark* (London and New York: Harper & Brothers, 1937), pp. 151 f., it is clear to me that Jesus may well have thought of himself as such. The question is whether the term in Jesus' day would have lent itself to such a use. Besides, how can we explain, on this basis, the fact that there is considerably more evidence in the Gospels that Jesus identified himself with the Son of Man than with the Messiah? In other words, I find myself agreeing with Branscomb's understanding of how Jesus conceived of his task (he was not simply another prophet), but am not convinced that he would have applied the term "Messiah" to himself or that, in fact, the evidence makes it at all probable that he did so. Branscomb's summary under the head, "Did Jesus regard himself as the Messiah?" (*op. cit.,* pp. 145 ff.), is excellent and important. See also C. T. Craig, "The Problem of the Messiahship of Jesus," in E. P. Booth, *New Testament Studies* (New York and Nashville: Abingdon-Cokesbury Press, 1942), pp. 95 ff.; and M. S. Enslin, "The Date of Peter's Confession," in *Quantulacumque* (London: Christophers', 1937), pp. 121 ff.

There is perhaps no really debatable question in the life of Jesus in which Christian theology and piety are likely to feel they have so much at stake as in this question of how Jesus regarded himself. For many the suggestion that Jesus may not have thought of himself as either Messiah or Son of Man may seem perilously near a denial of Christian faith in his supreme significance. Although the matter does not properly belong within an historical discussion, may I conclude this lecture with some remarks on this not unnatural state of mind.

The first remark is a reminder that the whole discussion turns on certain very specific patterns of thinking about God's agent in redemption. That any of these patterns could be in any literal sense accurate is exceedingly unlikely. It is not difficult to trace the development in history of the Jewish messianic conception and of the later Son of Man idea. The study of the origins and growth of these ideas is not likely to lead one to place unlimited confidence in their truth. Indeed, both cannot be true in any literal sense since they contradict each other at many points. As a matter of fact, it is a foregone conclusion that no human way of thinking about God and his ways can be literally accurate. "Messiah," "Son of Man" are human ways of thinking, historically developed, and at best can only point to, suggest, symbolize the final salvation, upon the reality of which faith and hope lay hold. In the literal sense Jesus could not have been the Messiah or the Son of Man because *in the literal sense* there is no Messiah or Son of Man. Why then should it seem so important that he should have thought of himself as such?

A second remark is the reminder that Jesus' significance does not at all depend upon the way he thought of himself. God did what he did in and through Jesus quite regardless of the terms in which Jesus conceived of his nature or task.

If the term " Christ " is used, not literally, to designate one who had been expected, but to designate him in whom the kingdom of God had actually been supremely revealed, then it can be believed that he was the " Christ." As we have seen, the primitive Christians, whatever Jesus' own view, confidently expected within their own genera‐ tion the fulfillment of the hopes of the prophets and apoca‐ lyptists and were sure that Jesus would shortly come again in glorious power to judge the world and to redeem the con‐ trite. Those expectations were disappointed; the fulfill‐ ment did not take place and Jesus did not come again. But the belief that he was the Christ cannot be dismissed as mere illusion. Jesus was called " Christ " not primarily because of what the early believers still hoped for from him but because of what they had actually found in him. In him they had already been confronted with the judgment of God; in him God's righteousness had already manifested itself as truth and grace.

He was the Christ, not because he inaugurated the king‐ dom in the apocalyptic sense or ever will (although it would be rash and presumptuous to affirm absolutely that he never will) , but because in him the eternal kingdom of God was in a unique and unprecedented way present and active within history, was not only seen and declared su‐ premely and unmistakably as righteousness and love, but was actually present as judgment and salvation. And though twenty centuries have passed, as we read his words and the meager story of his life and death and rising again, even we are made aware of the reality and the nearness of the kingdom of God. Even we can know that he was and is the Christ.

Lecture III

JESUS was remembered as a teacher of righteousness and there can be no question that the ethical teaching found in the Gospels of Matthew and Luke is based on, and fairly represents, this primitive memory. It is not necessary here to attempt any summary of this teaching — indeed, its characteristic tone and strength are largely lost in any paraphrase. The readers of these pages will be familiar with the more important sections of teaching material in the Synoptic Gospels, and I shall undertake no review of it.

The most striking feature of the ethical teaching of Jesus is the uncompromising nature of its demands. It is preoccupied with the absolutely good and spends little time with the better or the worse. Jesus had no time for dividing inheritances between brothers; he quickly disposes of a question about the propriety of paying taxes to Caesar; he has no interest in moral casuistry. His mind is fixed on the ultimate righteousness, and this he declares with matchless simplicity, serenity, majesty and grace.

This preoccupation of Jesus' ethical teaching with the absolutely good presents the interpreter with one of his most perplexing problems. The elements of the problem are two, both implicit in what has just been said. On the one hand, there is the difficulty posed by the extremeness, strenuousness, absoluteness of Jesus' interpretation of God's demands. Here such questions arise as: In what sense did Jesus intend such a saying as, " Give to him that asketh thee and from him that would borrow from thee

45

turn not thou away "? Did he mean that God actually demands so much of us, or did he mean only that God asks a
reasonable regard for others, the extreme form of the statement being merely rhetorical? If he really meant what
he said (and one is almost certain to decide that he did),
was his meaning determined and limited by his expectation of the imminent end of history, about which we were
thinking in the preceding lecture?

The other element in the problem consists in the apparent silence of Jesus on particular concrete questions of con-
duct and on the issue of what is better and what is worse in
situations where, given human finitude and sin and a fallen,
distorted world, perfect action is not possible. And here
again the question is bound to be asked whether this silence
is related to his eschatological expectations.

These two difficulties belong together as parts of one
problem, but the distinction between them is valid and,
for certain purposes (as, I believe, will shortly appear),
valuable. One difficulty grows out of the *presence* of something in Jesus' teaching, namely, a certain strenuous and
uncompromising quality; the other difficulty grows out of
the *lack* of something, namely, light on what particular
choices should be made between available alternatives in
many concrete situations. In one respect, the teachings say
too much; in the other, they say too little. On the one side
we read, " Sell whatsoever thou hast and give to the poor,
and thou shalt have treasure in heaven "; on the other,
" Who made me a judge or divider over you? "

To be sure, there are scholars who would take issue with
this statement about Jesus' silence and would claim that
his ethical teaching was intended primarily to apply to the
political situation in which his people found themselves
as vassals of Rome and that he was seeking to point a way

out of the disastrous impasse of war toward which he saw his country heading.[1] The absence, however, of any explicit reference to politics in Jesus' recorded teaching, although not decisive,[2] nevertheless creates a strong presumption against such an interpretation of his words. That he was aware of and sensitive to the political situation goes without saying; that he was on the whole silent about any particular technique for solving it seems likely. But how could he have been silent about a matter of such immense practical importance and of such deep ethical significance? Here is another instance of the second element in the problem we are considering.

The term " interim ethic " has been used in our brief discussion of Schweitzer's view of Jesus' thinking about the kingdom; it designates one important way of solving this problem. Those who take this way account for the extreme form in which Jesus' demands are stated and also for his silences by insisting that, dominated as he was by the expectation of the imminent catastrophe, his ethical teaching is concerned only with the short moment of historical existence which lay before that event. Not only did the times call for a kind of desperate righteousness, but such righteousness could appear feasible in such times — times so great and so short. Likewise, Jesus did not concern himself with questions of casuistry or of political strategy because such questions would so soon be utterly irrelevant. This world was passing away and its economic,

[1] This claim is advanced, for example, by V. G. Simkhovitch, *Toward the Understanding of Jesus* (New York: Macmillan Co., 1921) and by C. J. Cadoux, *The Historic Mission of Jesus* (London, 1941; New York: Harper & Brothers, 1943) .

[2] It may be argued that any such references would tend to drop out during the process of transmission, which took place, in its final, decisive stages, in a non-Palestinian environment, far removed from Jesus' own political problems.

social and political structures and habits were passing with it. In such a moment concern for all such things seemed trivial.

What are we to say about this interpretation of Jesus' ethical teaching? That it offers a plausible explanation of the two features of the teaching is obvious; and yet it falls short of being altogether convincing, chiefly because the manner of much of Jesus' most characteristic teaching is at the opposite pole from what one would expect to be the manner of a prophet giving a kind of desperate counsel for a moment of crisis. Words of Jesus which sound as though they had been uttered in such a mood can be found in the Gospels; but much of his ethical teaching is marked by the poise and serenity which suggest the sage and the long view rather than the prophet of an approaching crisis. Here is the issue between Schweitzer and Windisch [3] — and many others on both sides.

To this question of whether the ethic of Jesus was "eschatologically conditioned" I should say that no simple, "yes" or "no" answer can be given. Here, I suggest, appears the value of the distinction we have made between the positive and negative elements in the problem of Jesus' ethical teaching. If one is thinking about the negative element only — that is, about the silence of Jesus concerning particular questions of political organization and strategy or of moral casuistry — his belief in the early end of history may well be urged as the explanation. He is able to disregard many questions which must have appeared to his contemporaries as being of the utmost practical importance (as indeed they do to us also), because, as Jesus saw them, they belonged only to the brief interim before the

[3] See H. Windisch, *Der Sinn der Bergpredigt, Ein Beitrag zum Problem der richtigen Exegese* (Leipzig, 1929). Amos Wilder, in his *Eschatology and Ethics in the Teaching of Jesus* (New York: Harper & Brothers, 1939), makes an interesting and significant attempt to work out a synthesis.

kingdom should come.[4] In this view, the " interim " idea
is useful not in interpreting what Jesus said but in explaining why he did not say more.

As to what he *did* say — that is, as to his positive teaching about the will of God — it seems likely that although
it was related closely to his thinking about the coming kingdom, it was not in the usual sense eschatologically conditioned; indeed, quite the contrary. Jesus' ethic was a universal, not an " interim," ethic. Far from belonging to the
moment, it belonged to eternity. Jesus is concerned with
the absolute, pure will of God without compromise in view
of the conditions of human life and without concessions to
human finitude and sin.[5] The meaning of perfect goodness, it is safe to say, will never be seen more clearly nor described more adequately than he saw and described it. The
supreme greatness of Jesus as an ethical teacher does not lie

[4] I should be inclined to say that his silence about whether, and how,
evil ought directly to be dealt with can be so explained. I have tried to
state my views on this matter on pp. 38 ff. of a volume I had the honor of
editing several years ago, *Religion and the Present Crisis* (Chicago: University of Chicago Press, 1942) , and in an article in *Christianity and Crisis*
(March 8, 1943) . It seems to me that in discussions of ethics an important distinction needs to be made between the creation of good and
the restraint or destruction of evil. Now there can be no question that
Jesus was supremely interested in the growth of good. God is thought
of primarily as the Creator of good, and man's duty and destiny are seen
as fulfilled in cooperation with God in his work of love. Jesus' ethical
teaching is ideally adapted to this growth of good. Indeed, the only way
to make good grow is Jesus' way. Meekness, nonaggressiveness, complete
forgetfulness of self — this is the spirit in which alone the organic opera-
tion of creating good can be carried on. Rational critics of Jesus' ethical
teaching should recognize this: the end of ultimate importance is the
creation of good and Jesus' ethic is perfectly adapted to that end. It
does not follow, however, from Jesus' virtual silence about any human
responsibility for the restraint of evil, that he believed this result would
be attained as a kind of by-product of the growth of good. He undoubtedly believed that evil would have to be destroyed by direct means. God
would use these means — soon and with catastrophic results. His expectation of this act of God may well account for his not dealing with this part
of the ethical problem.

[5] I have found helpful Dibelius' statement on pp. 47 ff. of *The Sermon
on the Mount* (New York: Charles Scribner's Sons, 1940) .

in his skill as a casuist — that was a role he did not essay — but in his vision of the perfect will of God and in the clarity with which he saw that man in every moment of his existence is amenable to no standard short of that perfect will.

We often misunderstand Jesus because we are constantly doing our best to avoid recognition of this fact. The righteousness of God is so far beyond our capacity to achieve that in our pride we seek to forget it. We try to deceive ourselves into thinking that we owe no more than we can pay. God's righteousness requires that we deny ourselves; that we commit ourselves unreservedly, passionately, joyously to the good of others; that we be utterly true, simple, charitable and pure, not only in deed and word but also in the secret thoughts of our hearts. But finding that we are unable or unwilling to pay the price of such righteousness, we set up standards of our own. Instead of an impossible self-denial we set up a practicable self-restraint; instead of active self-sacrificial good will we set up a reasonable disinterestedness and are content if we hold self-love or national or class self-interest within moderate bounds; instead of an impossible purity, charity, and honesty of heart we set up a decent morality. And finding such standards practicable, we try to persuade ourselves that they represent not only all that we need to ask of ourselves or that others have a right to ask of us, but also all that God demands of us.

But as we listen to the ethical teachings of Jesus, all such pretenses are swept away. We sense the height, the depth and the breadth of the moral obligation under which we stand. We know we are judged not by the soft and easy standards we impose upon ourselves or the conventions of society impose on us, but by God's standards. The righteousness of God, which is ordinarily so hidden from us by our fears of others, our concern with trivialities, our rationalizations of our selfishness, that we think of it, if at all, as remote from us — this righteousness is revealed as bearing with its full and awful weight upon our lives with every breath we draw. With this perfect will Jesus confronted his own generation and has confronted inescapably every generation since.

Jesus as an ethical teacher belongs to all the generations just because he did not, in a sense, belong to his own. That is, the knowledge that he stood at or just before the final crisis of history allowed for a preoccupation with the absolute righteousness more complete and intensive than in ordinary circumstances might, humanly speaking, have been possible. If this is true, instead of blaming eschatology for the "impracticableness" of Jesus' ethical teaching, we should thank eschatology for that teaching's majesty and permanent relevance. Jesus' ethic was not an interim ethic — it was an absolute, universal ethic — but his clear vision of it was perhaps not unrelated to his expectation of the imminent coming of the kingdom. The vertical line relating man to the eternal order could be more clearly seen because the temporal horizontal line had become relatively so unimportant.

This vertical line is always there. Man always stands in this relation to the eternal and under the absolute obligation of love; but with history approaching its end, the absolute character of this moral obligation could appear extraordinarily stark and ominous. Jesus saw it with his whole mind and confronted his generation with its unreadiness for the coming crisis: "The kingdom of God is at hand; repent and believe the gospel."

The word "repent" is of the greatest importance in this passage and throughout Jesus' remembered teaching, for it is the answer to the inevitable question of one who is made aware of the height and depth of God's moral demands: " Who then can be saved? "

Paul, later, makes much of the distinction between " law " and " grace." Apparently he thought of these two terms as standing for two independent systems (so to speak) of salvation — " salvation " meaning reconciliation, restoration of fellowship with God. The apostle insists that if one is in the law system — that is, if one is relying upon obedience to God's commands for one's salvation — one's obedience must be complete. On the other hand, if one is relying upon God's forgiveness, or grace, no degree of mere obedience as such is required, only penitence and faith. Paul is convinced that the first alternative, salvation through perfect obedience, is purely hypothetical: no man can fulfill the requirement. He believes that in Christ, God opens to men the opportunity of fellowship with himself on other terms — terms which sinful, finite men can fulfill.

Now why does Paul, and the early church generally, associate with Jesus this opportunity of fellowship with God on the basis of penitence and faith? Why do they think of it as a new covenant which *Christ* has instituted? The answer must undoubtedly be that Jesus himself had brought home to the hearts of those who really heard his words that God stood ready to receive not simply the righteous — there was none righteous — but the penitent, those who acknowledged the absolute righteousness of God, felt the awful force of its demands upon them, realized how far short they fell of it, and with humble and contrite hearts sought his forgiveness and help. This was *not a new idea* in Israel; but Jesus saw so clearly its radical implications, gave himself to it so utterly, embodied it so movingly in his life and expressed it with such power and beauty in his words, that *a new thing had happened* in Israel. Jesus did not bring a new idea; rather, in him an old idea ceased being an idea at all and became a living reality. As he talked about the love of God, the love of God itself drew near.

It is possible to exaggerate the antinomy of grace and law, of penitence and obedience. This is true not only because penitence is possible only if one acknowledges the law and desires nothing so much as to fulfill it, but also because penitence inevitably issues in a renewed commitment to doing the will of God. Those whom Paul quotes (or imagines) as asking, " Shall we then sin that grace may abound? " showed that they did not know the meaning of grace — because they so obviously did not know the meaning of repentance. For penitence is a turning away from sin; and only the penitent can know the grace of forgiveness.

The ethical life which Jesus exalts in many of his most characteristic teachings is the ethical life of the penitent: the kingdom of God belongs to the poor in spirit, the meek, those who hunger and thirst after righteousness, those who seek mercy, the childlike, the humble. God asks perfect obedience — how can he ask less if he loves us? — but his love for us and the possibility of our entering into the enjoyment of his love do not depend upon our giving that measure of obedience. They depend only upon our submission to his will, our recognition of our moral need, and our trust in his forgiveness and help.

The righteousness which God requires of those who do *not* rely upon their righteousness is the righteousness of a contrite heart. Of those who *do* rely upon their righteousness God asks a righteousness far beyond their ability to achieve. " Those who are under the law are debtors to the whole law," Paul says on one occasion; and on another, " You are not under law, but under grace." These are Paul's words, and we cannot easily imagine them on Jesus' lips; but they say only what Jesus was remembered to have said over and over again in clearer, more concrete and more moving terms. For what else is the meaning of Jesus' constant use of the analogy of the family to set forth the realities of God's relation with us and of ours with him and with one another? A father's acceptance of his children does not depend upon the perfection of their obedience, but only upon their willingness to be filial. The Prodigal Son, who knows he is hardly worthy to be a slave in his father's house, can in virtue of that very fact be admitted to a more intimate and secure place in the family than his elder brother, who knows so little about what the obligations of the family are that he can imagine he has perfectly discharged a son's responsibilities and who knows so little about what the rewards of the family are that he can think of them as consisting in the privilege of eating a fatted calf!

Only by repentance, Jesus says, can one be ready for the kingdom, which is now coming with power. Only to those of humble and contrite heart can the rule of God in any sense belong.

We have already ceased dealing merely with the words of Jesus; and it is important to recognize that it was Jesus himself upon whom the church was based, not his words as such. His words might have been forgotten; but he would have been remembered. Indeed, there are those who hold that his words *were* forgotten; but, even if so, *he* was remembered. If he was not remembered to have spoken such words as are contained in the Sermon on the Mount, he was remembered to have been such a person as might have spoken them. If he was not remembered to have done any of the acts he is said to have performed, he was remembered to have been such a person as might have done them. If we could not trust any of the sayings or any of the deeds, we could still trust the impression of the sayer and the doer, which the Gospels convey. However much of what he did and said was forgotten, or half-forgotten, *he* was remembered by those who had been his disciples and associates and became the first Christian community.

He was remembered: but what was he remembered as being? One might attempt here some description of Jesus. But if the words of Jesus suffer in any paraphrase, the character of Jesus suffers even more in any description. It is noteworthy that although the New Testament is about Jesus, there is nowhere in it any description of him. The Gospels undertake only to tell us what he said and did, and we form our own impressions. His disciples remembered many things about him — we have been discussing through these three lectures what some of these things were — but the most important thing, so far as the beginnings of the church are concerned, was that they remembered him — remembered him in just the concrete, quite indescribable way we always remember persons we have known and loved.

I hope I may be forgiven a very personal illustration. The most vivid memory I have of a person, known long and well but long since, is of my father, a good minister of Jesus Christ, who died twenty years ago, almost to the day, as I write these words. He was a good father as well as a good minister, and my obligation to him is far beyond any possible calculation. But if I were asked to describe an incident in which my father took a significant part, I should have trouble recalling even one, and I am sure I could not in any case describe it fully or accurately. And although I listened to him speak, privately and publicly, on hundreds of occasions — and he had much that was original and important to say — I do not believe I could quote a single phrase from his lips or put into definite form a single idea I remember from him. And yet I remember him as though he were a part of myself — as indeed he is — and sometimes wake from sleep as though I had just heard his voice, or felt his hand, or seen him look at me.

So Jesus was remembered. We can be grateful that his disciples remembered as many words and incidents as they did. But we can be sure that they remembered *him* more vividly and more truly than any fact about him or anything he said. And it was that memory of Jesus himself upon which the Christian community, with all its life and faith, was in the first instance based. It was not primarily in his words or acts as such, but in himself, that the ineffable love of God made itself known as a living, potent and present reality.

It is not strange that this concrete meaning of Jesus for his disciples was forever and indissolubly associated in their minds with the terrible and tender events with which his life ended: the final meal dark with the forebodings of disaster, the hours in Gethsemane, the arrest, the brutal handling and the unjust trial, the unspeakable anguish, the long waiting for death, the final release. The whole meaning of Jesus for them came here to sharp and awful focus. Thenceforth to remember Jesus was to remember his cross; just as, later, to interpret Jesus was to interpret his cross. The cross became the central symbol of the church's faith only because it had first been the actual center around which the whole remembered meaning of the life of Jesus had been gathered.

Part Two

He Was Known Still

Lecture IV

IT IS not uncommon to distinguish between the Jesus of history and the Jesus of theology — between the " real " Jesus, who walked the ways of Palestine, and the beliefs about him which developed in the church — and to suppose that within those two terms the whole meaning of Jesus in the early church is contained. But that way of analyzing the early significance of Jesus leaves out of account what is in some ways its most important element. For Jesus was not merely remembered and interpreted in the primitive church: he continued to be known there. And the key to understanding both memory and interpretation is lost if that fact is forgotten.

The fact itself is unmistakable. The Gospels are concerned, formally, with Jesus as remembered, but one who reads with even half an eye cannot escape the fact that for the Gospel writers Jesus is not merely a person remembered; he is not even, primarily, a remembered person interpreted; he is a person still known who is both remembered and interpreted. This is most obviously true for the writer of the Fourth Gospel, but it is almost as clear for the other three. But what in the nature of the case can be only implicit in the Gospels is quite explicit in the letters of Paul and in other parts of the New Testament.

Paul rarely speaks of the man Jesus. Indeed, he does this so rarely that many students of his letters have decided that he was not at all concerned about the " historical Jesus "; some have gone so far as to affirm that he did not even know of his existence. Even the less extreme of these positions is false, as I hope I have shown: Christ for Paul was the *man* devotedly and reverently remembered in the community. But there can be no doubt that this man, thus remembered, was also known as a living, present reality. And it is as such that Paul usually speaks of him.   One could quote interminably from his letters in support of this point, but every reader of Paul will readily grant it.   Later in this lecture we shall be considering more exactly what this living, present Jesus meant to Paul.   At the moment we are concerned only with his reality.

There is every indication that Paul was not alone in thus regarding Jesus. The primitive church, for all its debt to the memory of Jesus, actually sprang out of the knowledge of him as alive after his passion. This fact every primitive strain in the New Testament makes quite clear. One may recognize that if Jesus of Nazareth had not been known and remembered in the company of his disciples, there could have been no knowledge of the resurrection, since in that case there would have been no one to receive that knowledge; but it is also true that without the knowledge of the resurrection the company of his disciples could never have become the Christian church.   The primitive Christian community was not a memorial society with its eyes fastened on a departed master; it was a dynamic community created around a living and present Lord.   Jesus was thought of the more tenderly because he had died; he continued to be thought of at all because he had risen again.

I have spoken of the resurrection as a fact, not as a belief; and we do not begin to think truly about it until we see it as such. The resurrection is a part of the concrete empirical meaning of Jesus, not the result of mere reflection upon that meaning. Beliefs were based upon the resurrection; it was not itself a belief. It was something given. It was a reality grasped in faith. It was the reality of all the concrete meaning of the man Christ Jesus recognized as present in the community after, and despite, his death. This knowledge of him as risen was as well established in the primitive community as was knowledge of him as a remembered person. And one could as well doubt the one as the other. The church, which remembered Jesus, also knew him still — and it would have seemed arbitrary to take the memory and to reject the knowledge. The New Testament is quite as sure that Jesus still lives — or lives again — as that he lived at all. The resurrection was part and parcel of the whole event we know as Jesus Christ, and made the same claim to be considered a fact as any other element in that event. Any grounds for rejecting the resurrection would have been grounds for rejecting the fact of Jesus himself.

In making such a statement, it is important to make clear at once that by the " fact of Jesus " I mean more than the merely formal, external fact that an individual by that name had actually lived at a given time and place. Obviously that fact could have been established on other grounds than those which also supported the fact of the resurrection. The bare " historicity " of Jesus could be " proved " in a way the resurrection could not be. But as I sought to show in the opening pages of this book, this merely formal fact, this bare " historicity," has no importance. The " fact of Jesus," in any important and really true sense, was Jesus as he was known and remembered in the community, and the testimony upon which we must rely for any knowledge of this fact must be taken as equally valid testimony to the resurrection. Thus one who denies *a priori* that there was objective ground for the resurrection faith of early Christianity denies in effect the whole Gospel portrait of Jesus, for the knowledge of the living Christ after the crucifixion is altogether continuous, of a piece, with the memory of the human Jesus.

It is also important to recognize that the real meaning and ground of the resurrection faith in the primitive church was not particular items in the tradition nor particular views as to how Christ's victory over death was accomplished. On this latter point various views were bound to develop, and these views, as well as the legendizing tendency, which is never absent from a growing tradition, were certain to affect the way in which the *story* of the resurrection was told. But the resurrection faith at no time rested upon a story; it would be less false — although that does not mean it would be true — to say that the story rested upon the faith. The resurrection faith rested upon something given within the community's experience. The situation in the early church was not that Jesus was believed to be living because he was believed to have risen; it was rather that he was known to have risen because he was known as living.

As far as they go, the " story " of the resurrection and the formal evidence marshaled to support it tend to sustain this view. That evidence is of two kinds: the appearances of Jesus to his disciples and the empty tomb. There can be no doubt as to which is the more primitive. The earliest surviving " defense " of the fact of the resurrection is that of Paul in I Corinthians. He cites the evidence which he had received:

He [Jesus] was seen by Cephas, then by the twelve. After that he was seen by more than five hundred brethren at once, of whom the greater part remain until this present, but some are fallen asleep. After that he was seen by James, then by all the apostles.[1]

Paul does not mention the finding of the empty tomb, and it may be safely presumed that he does not know of it. Why otherwise should he omit so impressive a fact?

But if Paul recounts appearances but says nothing about

[1] I Cor. 15:5 ff.

the empty tomb, Mark, our next earliest source, tells of the empty tomb, but does not describe any appearances.[2] This does not mean either that Mark does not know about appearances or that he regards the empty tomb as intrinsically more impressive evidence of the resurrection. The young man arrayed in a white robe (presumably an angel) whom the women see in the open sepulcher tells them to say to Jesus' disciples that they will see their Master in Galilee. There can be no doubt whatever that Mark knew (and knew his readers knew) that this promise had been fulfilled. Mark does not need to recount the appearances themselves: they were too well known. Like the good dramatist he was, he only points to them, preferring to end his book with the marvelously impressive fact which had only recently made its way into the tradition, or, if earlier, had not become widely known — the empty tomb.

There are, besides Paul's omission of this item, at least two other grounds for regarding it as relatively late, both of which appear when we compare Mark with the later Gospels. The first of these is the secrecy surrounding the empty tomb in Mark. The only persons who witnessed it said " nothing to anyone; for they were afraid." Here is Mark's way of explaining why so striking a fact had not been known from the beginning. But when the later Gospels were written, the generation which had known the primitive tradition at first hand had passed, and the empty tomb seemed as early as any other part of the tradition. The explanation was no longer needed. This appears clearly when we compare the last three verses of Mark with

---

[2] I do not share the suspicion, which goes back to ancient times, that Mark did not originally end with 16:8. The matter is fully discussed by R. H. Lightfoot in *Locality and Doctrine in the Gospels* (London and New York: Harper & Brothers, 1938), pp. 1–48. To the earlier literature of the subject to which Lightfoot refers I would add the important article of Martin Rist, " Is Mark a Complete Gospel? " in the *Anglican Theological Review*, XIV (1932), 143 ff.

the corresponding section of Matthew. The writer of Matthew is closely following Mark up to the middle of the last verse, but at that point he departs radically from his source:

MARK (16:6–8)	MATTHEW (28:5–8)
And he [the " young man "] saith unto them, Be not afraid: ye seek Jesus of Nazareth, who was crucified: he is risen; he is not here; 'behold the place where they laid him. And go your way, tell his disciples and Peter that he goeth before you into Galilee: there shall ye see him, as he said unto you. And they went out quickly, and fled from the sepulcher; for they trembled and were amazed: neither said they anything to anyone; for they were afraid.	And the angel answered and said unto the women, Fear not ye: for I know that ye seek Jesus, who was crucified. He is not here: for he is risen, as he said. Come, see the place where the Lord lay. And go quickly, and tell his disciples that he is risen from the dead; and, behold, he goeth before you into Galilee; there ye shall see him: lo, I have told you. And they departed quickly from the sepulcher with fear and great joy; and ran to bring his disciples word.

Mark's Gospel manifestly appeared at a time when such a question might be asked as: " Why did we not hear of this finding of the empty tomb before? I heard Paul once, and a friend of mine once heard Peter, but we heard nothing of this." Mark answers: " They said nothing to anyone: for they were afraid." The question had become impossible and the answer unnecessary when Matthew and the other Gospels were written.

The same significance belongs to the fact that in Mark only certain obscure women see the empty tomb. It was Peter, James, John and other well known disciples of Jesus who were remembered to have first preached the resurrection. But they had spoken only of appearances, it was recalled, not of the empty tomb. This, Mark says in effect, was only because none of them had known of it. That knowledge was given only to some women and they, as we have seen, said nothing about it. But again, the explanation is not needed a little later. And so in Luke we are told that " certain of those who were with us " (24:24) also visited the empty tomb, and in the Fourth Gospel, more definitely, that Peter and another disciple saw it.

The purpose of these remarks is not to discredit the story of the finding of the empty sepulcher (although it cannot be denied that serious doubt is cast on it), but rather to point out that the primitive evidence for the resurrection was the actual presence of Jesus. The resurrection was not an inference from the empty tomb; if anything, the empty tomb was a later inference from the known fact of Christ living after his passion. Since he was alive, he must have left the sepulcher.

I have already cited the list of appearances to which Paul appeals. With this most primitive list others only partly agree. In Mark, as we have seen, there are no appearances. In Matthew, Jesus appears to Mary Magdalene, " the other Mary," and the eleven. In Luke, he appears to the two disciples going to Emmaus, to Simon, and to the eleven. In John, he is seen by Mary Magdalene, by the eleven except Thomas, by the eleven with Thomas, and by several disciples at the Sea of Tiberias. The harmonizing of these lists is quite impossible. There are obvious reasons for trusting Paul's as the most authentic, but there is no sufficient ground for placing unlimited confidence even in its accuracy. But the accuracy of such accounts is really unimportant. The knowledge of the resurrection never rested upon such accounts only or as such; it rested upon what was recognized to be the presence of Jesus within the community. It is significant in this connection that although Paul recounts the appearances which he has " received " and expects the Corinthians to be impressed by this evidence, nevertheless he did not himself accept the fact of the resurrection until Jesus appeared to him also. Many to whom such appearances were not vouchsafed were aware of the presence of the Lord Jesus in the fellowship. It was in the experience of that spiritual reality that the faith of the resurrection really consisted.

Must not this be Paul's meaning in those frequently debated words, " The Lord is the Spirit "? It is sometimes claimed that Paul is here using the term " Lord " in its Septuagint sense to refer to Yahweh or God. That obviously is possible, but seems hardly probable. Paul pretty consistently reserves the title " Lord " for Jesus, to whom he tells us God expressly gave it at the moment of the resurrection and exaltation. I believe that in this disputed passage the apostle is simply identifying the Lord Jesus with the Spirit, known in the Christian fellowship. He can call this Spirit the " Spirit of Christ," the " Spirit of Jesus Christ," the " Spirit of the Lord," or the " Spirit of the Son of God." [3] Why can he not also say, " The Lord *is* the Spirit," or " The Spirit is the Lord "? Here is adumbrated the doctrine of the relation of Christ and the Spirit which the Fourth Gospel was to state more explicitly:

I will pray the Father and he will give you another Helper, that he may abide with you forever; even the Spirit of truth, whom the world cannot receive because it seeth him not, neither knoweth him; but ye know him; for he dwelleth with you and shall be in you. I will not leave you comfortless: I will come to you. Yet a little while and the world seeth me no more; but ye shall see me. (14:16 ff.)

Here Christ is identified with the Spirit. This is no late development in Christian reflection; it might be truer to say that such an identification cannot bear much reflec-

[3] In I Cor. 15:45, Paul says, speaking of Christ, " The last Adam was made a quickening Spirit."

tion — which is one reason for the later elaboration of the doctrine of the Trinity. This identification of the risen, living Christ with the Spirit goes back to the moment of the church's creation. The church was born of the Spirit; and that Spirit was from the beginning recognized to be the presence and power of the living Jesus. It is in that fact (not in any appearances, merely as such) that the resurrection faith was securely based.

And it is based there still, and will always be. Our faith in the resurrection is far more — indeed, radically other — than acceptance of the ancient accounts of Jesus' appearances to his disciples. There is no reason to reject these accounts. However one may conceive of the psychological character of these experiences, there can be no doubt that they occurred. But such appearances by themselves prove nothing: they may be explained in purely subjective terms. As a matter of fact, we are certain to explain them so unless we ourselves " know him and the power of his resurrection." [4] But if we do thus know him, we cease to have *a priori* either any ground for doubting the objective character of the appearances as such or any imperious reason for maintaining it. For if our faith in the resurrection has any vitality or validity, it is nothing less than the conviction that there is even now present and knowable within the Christian fellowship through " the Holy Spirit, which is given unto us," the full concrete personal meaning of " Jesus Christ and him crucified." This is a mystery — yea, a miracle — but to deny it means denying not only what is essential and central in the Christian theological position but also what has been for twenty centuries the most intimate and secure conviction of Christian devotion. No one can hope to understand the New Testament or the early church who begins by assuming that this con-

4 Phil. 3:10.

viction was mistaken. The early church's knowledge of
the living Christ cannot be separated, except by the most
arbitrary procedures, from its knowledge of the crucified
Jesus. The same person who was remembered was known
still.

When we inquire further as to the concrete meaning of
Jesus, after his death, within the life of the early Christian
community, we find ourselves at once forced to deal with
two theological issues of fundamental importance: the nature of the church and the nature of revelation; for the
essential and permanent significance of Jesus lies in the
fact that he was the center and head of the church and
that he was the central figure in that revelation of God
which we have received and by which we are saved. In
other words, he was, as Acts says, " both Lord and Christ."
We do not need to share the apocalyptic faith of the primitive church to understand and accept this statement. The
rest of this lecture will be devoted to elaborating it.

I spoke just now of the nature of the church and the
nature of revelation as being two issues, but they are so
closely related to each other that they may almost be dealt
with as one. Certainly they cannot be treated separately.
This is true because of the double-sided fact that the revelation took place within the church and the church was
constituted by the revelation: without the church there
could have been no revelation, but without the revelation
the church itself could not have come into being.

When we say that without the church there could have
been no revelation, we mean, to speak more accurately,
that there could have been no revelation without a community prepared to receive it. This follows partly from
the fact that revelation has by definition a subjective as

well as an objective side. To reveal something is to make it known — that is, known by someone else. Even God could not reveal what is not seen, any more than he could give what is not received. But involved also in this recognition of the intimate connection of revelation and the church is the fact that the primary medium of revelation, according to both Christian and Hebrew understanding, is events, not words, and that the content of revelation is God himself, not ideas (however true) about God.

This understanding of revelation is of the greatest importance for our thinking about many matters. It offers the key, for example, to a true evaluation of the Bible. The Bible is not itself the revelation of God; it is the record or report of the revelation. It is a human book and has in it the marks of human finitude and sin. But, for all that, it is absolutely irreplaceable and is of supreme and unique importance. This is true, not because it contains, as it does, more exalted religious ideas than any other book, or expresses them better (this would be an explanation of the Bible's superiority, not of its uniqueness), but because it stands in a unique relation to some unique and supremely significant events. The Bible is an account of some events in which God acted to make himself known, as those events happened (that is, as they were received and understood) within the community of Israel and, later, the community of Christ. It is thus, paradoxically, both less and greater than the church. It is less than the church because it is a product of the church and can be understood only in the context which the life of the church provides; it is greater than the church because it is, by and large, the only record we have of the events which not only brought the church into being but also through which its reality must be continually renewed. The Bible is not most truly described as being the Word of God, or even as " containing " the Word of God; rather, it points to, is a response to, the Word of God. For the Word of God is not a word at all (much less a vast number of words) ; it is an act. The revelation of God is God himself acting within events and making himself known to those who are able to witness the events (and therefore among whom alone they can happen) as a concrete, ineffable Reality.

" Making himself known," I say; not imparting truths about himself. The revelation of the grace of God, for example, is not the disclosure of the *truth that* God is gracious; it is God disclosing *himself as* gracious. There is all the difference between the abstract and the concrete, between ideas and reality, in these two statements.

To be sure, ideas are certain to be associated with the revelation. But the ideas, merely as such, are ours, not God's. God's thoughts are not our thoughts, and even revelation cannot make them so. Our religious ideas are our ways of interpreting the Reality, which alone is given in revelation. Archbishop Temple writes:

Faith is not the holding of correct doctrines, but personal fellowship with the living God. Correct doctrines will both express this, assist it and issue from it; incorrect doctrine will misrepresent this and hinder or prevent it. Doctrine is of an importance too great to be exaggerated, but its place is secondary, not primary. I do not believe in any creed, but I use certain creeds to express, to conserve, and to deepen my belief in God. What is offered to man's apprehension in any specific revelation is not truth concerning God, but the living God Himself.[5]

---

[5] *Nature, Man and God* (London and New York: Macmillan Co., 1935) , p. 322. See also Temple's essay in the symposium, edited by John Baillie and Hugh Martin, *Revelation* (Glasgow and New York: Macmillan Co., 1937) , from which I quote the following paragraph: " What is the nature of the ' object ' in which the revelation is offered? Is it a Truth? — that is, something primarily belonging to the ' subject ' though having application to the object world. Or to put the question in another way, does God chiefly give his revelation by introducing ideas — whether convictions or determinations — into the mind of the prophet, or by guiding

Now Jesus Christ is an event in and through which " the living God Himself " is offered for our apprehension.[6] Sometimes Christian scholars have been greatly exercised to prove that in Christ we have a new *conception* of God. It is a hard point to make and is of doubtful truth. But whether true or not, the significance of Jesus in revelation does not depend upon it. The revelation of God in Christ is not the imparting of a new idea of God; it is a fresh unveiling of the Reality to which ideas, new and old, with greater or less adequacy, apply.

This can be illustrated from the teaching of Jesus. Controversy has often been waged around the question of the originality of Jesus' teaching. Did Jesus introduce new ideas about God, about the meaning of human life and history, about man's ethical obligations, or were his ideas derived from his Jewish heritage? Many Christian interpreters, feeling that an issue of critical importance was involved in that question, have defended the originality of Jesus' ideas as though they were protecting the most precious tenet of their faith. Other interpreters, however, both Jewish and

---

external events in which the prophet sees His hand? The question is of great practical importance for religion. For if God chiefly follows the way of introducing ideas, then revelation itself can be formulated in propositions which are indubitably true. But if He chiefly follows the way of guiding external events [and this, needless to say, is Temple's view], these constitute the primary vehicle of the revelation; and events cannot be fully formulated in propositions; the event is always richer than any description of it " (pp. 100 ff.) . (Both of these quotations are made by permission of the Macmillan Company, publishers.)

The same view is expressed in the very beautiful and moving book by John Baillie, *Our Knowledge of God* (New York: Charles Scribner's Sons, 1939) . Baillie writes (p. 175) : " Revelation essentially consists not in the communication of truths about God but in the self-revelation of the divine Personality, the truths about Him being abstracted by ourselves from the concrete reality with which we thus become acquainted." (Quoted by permission of Charles Scribner's Sons, publishers.)

[6] Is not this near to what the Fourth Gospel is saying in 5:39: " Ye search the Scriptures for in them ye think ye have eternal life, but these are they that testify of me, and ye will not come to me that ye may have life "?

non-Jewish, locating " parallels " to all of Jesus' teachings (taken severally) in Hebrew or Jewish literature, have denied his originality and, by implication, the reality of any new revelation in him. Many exceptions could be taken to each position; but both are alike wrong in this: both presuppose a false conception of the meaning of revelation. Both assume that it consists in the imparting of new ideas. Now, as I had occasion to hint in an earlier lecture, Jesus did not bring new ideas in the formal sense: the oneness, holiness and ultimate sovereignty of God, his love and care for all his creatures, his requirement of righteousness, his willingness to receive the penitent, our duty of compassion toward all men, especially the needy and helpless — these ideas, merely as ideas, were familiar within Judaism. Why should we expect that this would not be true, or want it otherwise? To be sure, Jesus presented these ideas — especially some of them — with a new emphasis and with a new grace and power; and if the particular manner in which ideas are conceived and expressed is taken into account, the originality of Jesus' mind is manifest to all but the least discerning. But the greatest significance of Jesus as a teacher does not lie in the novelty of his ideas or even in the new ways in which he felt and expressed old ideas.

That significance lies in the undeniable fact that the God who " made known his ways unto Moses, his acts unto the children of Israel," revealed himself as a concrete reality afresh in and through the words of this man, who " spoke as never man spoke." As Jesus spoke, ideas became vital and concrete; what had been for many merely formal truth became living reality. Men who had long known *that* God was righteous, knew, as they listened, the reality of God *as* righteous. Men who were familiar with the *idea* that God was merciful and would receive the penitent, realized that in Jesus God *was being* merciful and *was receiving* the penitent. The words of Jesus were a part of the deed of God.

And if this is true of his words, it is much more clearly true of his whole life as a person. In and through him God manifested himself afresh in a mighty creative (and therefore redemptive) act. It was not a new God who thus acted, or an unknown God; it was the God who had called the Hebrew community into existence and had revealed himself continuously in the history of the Jewish nation. That same God revealed himself again — and supremely. However we explain it, the God of all righteousness and love *did* make himself known with mighty, unprecedented power in Jesus — living, dying, risen — and arguments about the novelty of this or that element in his teaching do not touch the point at all.

But Jesus did not live in a vacuum; he lived in a community: the larger community of Israel, and the smaller, more intimate community which formed itself about him and of which he was himself a part. If that group had not been formed, not only would the revelation not have been perpetuated, it could not have taken place at all. What we have in the Gospels is not merely Jesus as he was, but Jesus as he was known in the circle of his associates and their successors. It was in Jesus *as known in the church,* both before his death and afterwards, that the fresh activity of God among men, which we call the revelation in Christ, first occurred. It was in the fellowship that men had with Jesus and with one another around Jesus — living, dying, and alive for evermore — that God drew wondrously near as grace and truth.[7]

---

[7] In my own thinking about these matters I have been greatly indebted to my friend, Charles Clayton Morrison. His book, *What Is Christianity?* (Chicago: Willett, Clark & Co., 1940), lays a powerful emphasis upon the concrete character of revelation and contains any number of passages in which that idea is presented with extraordinary bril-

But if it is true that there could have been no revelation without the church, it is also true that there would have been no church without the revelation. The revelation constituted the church. As the revelation progressed, the community became more and more distinctively the church.

---

liancy of conception and style. May I further emphasize and clarify the point I am endeavoring to make by quoting two of them:

"The revelation of God in history is not the dictation of truth to men's minds; it is divine action in the communal field of events. For history is just this field or continuum of events. Revelation is not a truth uttered, but a deed done. God does not perform the deed and in addition dictate man's response to the deed. If that were the method of his revelation, we should have to charge God with arbitrary favoritism in revealing himself to one particular community rather than to another. Indeed, if this were God's way of revealing himself, there could be no reason why he should not reveal himself to all mankind simultaneously. But this is not God's way. Revelation presupposes as its complement the human capacity and disposition to receive the revelation. And this involves man's freedom and intelligence. In revealing himself, God does not violate the freedom of man's will or of his intelligence. Here as everywhere he stands at man's door and knocks. In all revelation there is a divine part and there is a human part, an event or an activity and an interpretation or a response. The living community which has once made a corporate response to the divine revelation does so with an ideology of its own, and it approaches each new revelatory event with an ideology which is as human in its origin and nature as any body of human thought can be. The ideology is man's contribution to the concrete revelation. . . . God's revelation does not consist of any absolute deposit of divine truth of which the community bearing the divine revelation is the custodian. The *community* is the divine revelation, because *it* is the creative work of God " (pp. 59-60) .

"Not the Bible, but the living church, the body of Christ, is the true Word of God. His Word is not an idea, nor a body of ideas, nor a book containing ideas: God's Word is God's *deed*. It is not man's commentary on God's deed, nor man's commentary on his human experience of God's deed. The Word of God is the deed itself, the actual creative working of God in a specific order of human community in which he has revealed himself in history " (p. 208) .

I find myself unable to accept Dr. Morrison's thesis at only one point, although that is a point which, I fear, he would regard as an important one. It seems to me that his absolute identification of the revelation with the church is not accurate: I would say that the revelation took place within the church and is inconceivable apart from it, but I find it impossible to say, as he frequently does, that the revelation *is* the church. But this difference, which may be less real and important than I think, does not obscure my appreciation of the truth and brilliance of Dr. Morrison's discussion of the concreteness of revelation and of its inseparable connection with the community.

A good case could be made for the view that the church began when Israel began and that it will not be truly itself until the kingdom of God shall have come. But one can hardly doubt that there have been two supreme moments in the life of the Christian church: one was the moment when Jesus called about him a company of disciples, and the other, the moment when, after his death, he became known to them as alive and with them forever. If I were forced to name one or the other of these two moments as that in which the Christian church in its distinctive character began, I should probably name the second of them, for it was only then that the community became fully conscious of itself. But the resurrection could not have occurred if the church in some real sense had not already come into existence. For the resurrection was not simply Jesus alive after his passion; it was Jesus alive and also known and accessible within the community prepared to recognize and receive him.

He was known there as Savior and Lord. Although a discussion of these terms as they were used in the early church may appear to belong more appropriately later, when we shall be considering specifically how Jesus was interpreted, some attention to their meaning is necessary here. For underneath all the explanations of why and how men might be saved through Christ was the fact that they were actually saved through him. And underneath all the interpretations of Jesus' lordship was the fact that he was in truth the Lord. May I speak briefly of both of these terms, reserving fuller discussion for later chapters.

First, then, Jesus was known as Savior. I do not mean that he was called by that name: he may have been, or may not have been, at any particular time or place. I mean that the revealing act of God within the life of the community, which, as we have seen, was recognized as being continuous with what took place through the life and words of Jesus and which could be referred to as " Christ," or " the Spirit," or in other ways — this act was a saving act. The perennially deepest needs of men are for forgiveness and for new life. Men are not always aware of this fact — which suggests, as Paul explains, the function and value of law in the spiritual life. But the need is persistent and universal. Man is in bondage to sin and to death, unable either to justify himself or to emancipate himself. This was true in the first century — and among Jews as well as Greeks — as it is true still. Now the simple, but miraculous, fact was that within the early Christian community forgiveness and moral renewal were actually found. Men knew themselves to be forgiven and to have been brought into a new relationship with God in which moral resources were available to them of which they had not dreamed before. They had received the " adoption." A new Spirit within them (not their own, and yet more intimately and truly theirs than if it had been their own) cried, " Abba, Father! " This Spirit bore witness within them that they were the sons and heirs of God. All of this had happened " through Christ." This was " the power of his resurrection."

The reason this effect followed upon Jesus' life and death was a matter for reflection and speculation, as we shall see; but the effect itself was a fact of immediate experience. Because of the events summed up and designated in the term " Christ " (that is, Jesus remembered and still known) , the whole situation of man in his relation with God (and therefore with himself and his fellows) had been profoundly changed. Reconciliation (atonement, community) was possible as it had not been possible before. Jesus was the Savior.

He was also the Lord. The Greek term " Lord " is highly ambiguous, as were also the corresponding Aramaic terms. In its primary meaning the term referred to anyone with authority over another, as, for example, the master of a slave; but use in many connections had greatly enriched that original meaning: the word might be employed as a simple title of respect, much like our " Sir," or it might occur in an address to God. In the sacramental mystery cults, which were so influential in the Mediterranean world of the first century, the term (or its equivalent, " Lady ") was regularly used to designate the deity who was believed to preside over the cult. It has often been argued that the Christian application of the word to Jesus derives from this pagan practice. It would be natural to suppose that early Gentile Christians, familiar with the mystery cults — perhaps even former members of one or another of them — would interpret the lordship of Jesus in ways determined, at least in part, by their previous experiences. But there is every indication that the term " Lord " was in use within the church before Gentiles in large numbers came in and therefore before the influence of the mysteries could have been felt.[8]

The fact that the term had been used to translate the name of Yahweh in the Septuagint also undoubtedly had its effect. We have already observed that from quite early times the Christians were accustomed to read occurrences of " the Lord " in the Greek Scriptures as allusions to Christ. But again, it is clear that the use of the title " Lord " as applied to Jesus did not originate in this way, since he was apparently first called by that name in Palestine itself,

---

8 See S. J. Case, " Κύριος as a Title for Christ," *Journal of Biblical Literature*, XXVI (1907) , 151 ff.; and *The Evolution of Early Christianity*, pp. 116 ff. See also B. W. Bacon, " Jesus as Lord," in *Jesus the Son of God* (New Haven: Yale University Press, 1911) , pp. 53 ff.; and, on the other side, W. Bousset, *Kyrios Christos* (Göttingen, 1913) .

where the Bible was read in Hebrew and the Septuagint was unknown.

Whatever technical theological connotations the term "Lord" acquired, its original intention was to acknowledge Jesus Christ as the Master of life and the center and head of the community. No reader of the New Testament can miss the fact that such in very truth he was. His remembered words and example had unquestionable authority. His will as it made itself known to the community was final and decisive. Devotion to him was the very life of the church. The community offered its prayers and adoration to him, and knew that in doing so it was offering them through him to God.

Principal Jacks has used as the title of one of his stimulating little books on the religious life the phrase, "the lost radiance of the Christian religion," and no one, I dare say, would need to read the book to know what that phrase is intended to convey. For if anything is clear to the average modern Christian with even a casual knowledge of the New Testament, it is, first, that "radiant" is hardly the word he would think of to describe his own religious life or that of his contemporaries, and secondly, that no other term characterizes so well the life of the primitive church. According to one of the Gospels, Jesus said to his disciples just before the crucifixion, "My joy I leave with you." Whether he made such a promise or not, there can be no doubt of its fulfillment. Among the most striking characteristics of the earliest Christian communities was their joy, their radiant sense of adequacy. They had overcome the world.

This joyous consciousness of victory pervades in every

part the documents which the early church produced and in which its life is reflected. Scores of passages come to our minds: " Joy unspeakable and full of glory "; " Blessed be the Lord God of Israel, for he hath visited and redeemed his people "; " Thanks be to God who giveth us the victory "; " Mine eyes have seen thy salvation "; " We are more than conquerors "; " We rejoice in the hope of the glory of God "; " Thanks be to God for his unspeakable gift "; " Thanks be to God who causeth us to triumph in Christ "; " God who commanded the light to shine out of darkness hath shined in our hearts." These are only a few of the passages in which the early community attempted to express a shared experience which lay beyond the power of language to describe. It *was* joy unspeakable. And in the power of that joy they went forth to possess a world which they believed had already been conquered for them.

When one seeks the ground of this joyous confidence, one does not find it, needless to say, in any outward circumstance or in any spectacular achievement. To the average intelligent pagan of the first century, if we might assume for a moment that he was acquainted with any of the scattered churches, nothing could have seemed more absurd than the happiness of these Christians, not many of whom, as Paul says, were wise, mighty or noble. It was not their numbers, wealth, social position, nor their intellectual or moral virtue, which made of a dozen or so discouraged disciples of a slain and discredited leader the most creative group in human history, a living fire which set the whole Mediterranean world aflame.

If we had asked the early Christians themselves about the source of their joy and power, they would have answered without any hesitation that it lay not in themselves at all — not in their attainments, not even in their faith — but in

God. " *God* hath visited and redeemed his people." A new epoch in human history has begun, they would have said; the God of all creation has manifested himself in mighty acts of righteousness and mercy. Because of these acts we know him to be real, accessible, and infinitely gracious, and in that knowledge we find the promise of both the coming of his kingdom and the ultimate fulfillment of our own lives: " Through the tender mercy of our God, the day-spring from on high hath visited us, to give light to them that sit in darkness and in the shadow of death, to guide our feet into the way of peace." [9] It was not something they had thought, but something God had done, which the first Christian preachers proclaimed.

Evidences of this gracious and mighty activity of God they would have found abundantly in the history of Israel. But it had occurred supremely in an event of which they were themselves witnesses, Jesus Christ the Lord. As we shall see, they may well have differed in the terms they used to interpret this experience — certainly Christians a little later did — but of the experience itself they would have had no doubt: God had come near in Christ. He had manifested himself clearly, unmistakably, powerfully, in the life of this man, whom their own eyes, strange to say, had seen; whom their own hands, incredibly, had touched; and whom now they knew as a divine reality within the fellowship which he had called into being and of which he was the head and center.

This awareness of the actual presence of the love and power of God as manifested in Christ is the " radiance of the Christian religion." In so far as it has been lost, the church has become futile and impotent. The recovery of it means something more and other than a return to the terms and symbols of the New Testament. It means a

[9] Luke 1:78 f.

fresh apprehension of the working of God in history: a fresh and vivid realization of the God who in Christ revealed himself to men long ago and who, still in Christ, stands ready to make himself known in gracious power also to us and to our generation.

Part Three

He Was Interpreted

So FAR we have been thinking principally about the concrete meaning of Jesus. The early church held in its heart the memory of Jesus and the experience of his continuing and saving reality. But the early church, like everything else human, was mind as well as heart, and almost at once was seriously engaged in the attempt to *understand* this concrete meaning: "Why is Jesus so important? Why does he mean so much? How does it happen that we are saved through him?" The final two lectures in this series will be concerned with such questions as these — that is, with the way or ways in which the primitive church interpreted and explained the meaning of Jesus. In this lecture we shall be considering the question, "Who was this Jesus?" and in the following one, the question, "What did he do for man?" We cannot hope in two lectures to cover with even passable adequacy the whole field of Christology (not to speak of soteriology) in the early church. We shall perforce give most attention to Paul, its most articulate and most influential theologian, but we shall attempt to indicate, at least, the ways in which other writers of the New Testament (and presumably the communities for which they spoke) diverged from his position.

The most primitive interpretation of Jesus is undoubtedly represented by the assertion ascribed to Peter in Acts 2:36: "God hath made this same Jesus whom ye crucified both Lord and Christ." [1] We can be sure that this inter-

---

[1] For one who, as I do, regards Luke-Acts as being in its final form relatively late — that is, a second-century work — it may seem arbitrary

pretation marks the very beginning of reflection because, as we were trying to say in the preceding lecture, it closely approximates to being a mere description of what the community actually knew in its experience. So far as the affirmation of Jesus' lordship is concerned, the barest minimum of interpretation is involved. " This same Jesus " was the man whom the community remembered; he is now known as " Lord." The Acts account of the primitive preaching (at least as regards the lordship of Jesus) is not so much a theological interpretation of Jesus as the affirmation of what the early church had found him to be. " Jesus is Lord " was not the conclusion of a syllogism; it was a fact given in the life of the community. This is what Paul means when he says, " No one can say Jesus is Lord except by the Holy Spirit." [2]

The assertion in the Acts source that he has also been made " Christ " involves a larger element of purely rational interpretation. In this passage it probably means no more than that " this same Jesus " has been designated God's agent in judging the world and inaugurating the new age, an office which he will soon " return " (that is, appear in visible form) to fulfill. The meaning of the concept of messiahship as applied to Jesus must occupy us, at least briefly, later in this discussion. Just now I am concerned only with the two points: that the first answer to the query, " Who was this Jesus?," was simply, " He was a man whom

---

to single out such a passage as this as representing a really primitive view. But whenever Luke-Acts, as we have it, was composed, there can be no doubt that it was based upon earlier sources, and, unfortunately, the grounds for a decision as to what is earlier and what is later have not been established by literary criticism, perhaps cannot ever be. But whether Acts 2:36 belongs to a primitive source of Acts or not, the passage must be taken as setting forth a primitive view, for the reason which I go on to state above. The writer either had a primitive source here or a sound historical understanding of what would have been the Christology of the first believers.

[2] I Cor. 12:3.

many of us knew and loved, whom God has now raised from
the dead and exalted to the right hand of his power "; and
that this answer, often called " adoptionism," was inevitably the first answer to the question, because it included
little if anything beyond what was actually given in the
life of the early church — the man Jesus remembered
simply as a man, and his continuing presence in and above
the community as the divine Lord, the resurrection mark-
ing the moment when the transformation was accomplished.

If this first answer to the so-called christological question
stands forth fairly clearly, so also does the final answer, to
which the church of the New Testament period was early
inclined and gradually came. It is the answer stated most
fully and unqualifiedly in the Fourth Gospel. This answer
begins with an affirmation of the pre-existence of Jesus:
When Jesus ascended to the Father after his resurrection
(for by the end of the first century, or soon afterward, resurrection and exaltation, originally one event, have been
distinguished from each other [3]), he merely resumed a place
which he had never really relinquished. For he was the
eternal Wisdom or Logos of God. He was God's agent in
creation: " all things were made through him and without
him was nothing made that was made." [4] He was the eter-

[3] It hardly needs to be pointed out that there is no ascension in Paul.
The risen Christ is, as such, the exalted Christ. The " appearances " of
Jesus after his death are appearances not only of the risen but also of the
glorified Redeemer. But these appearances did not continue to occur
(Paul says that the appearance to him was as to " one born out of due
time ") ; and by the end of the first century it was possible to think of
them as having been confined to the short and definite period after the
resurrection of which the final exaltation, or ascension, marked the end.
Notice that Paul thinks of the appearance to him as having been of exactly
the same character as to Cephas, James, and the rest (I Cor. 15:5 ff.) , but
the author of Luke-Acts (a half-century or more later) thinks of it as
having occurred after the ascension and as being therefore of a very different, a more " heavenly," character.

[4] John 1:3.

nal Son of God, not in the merely functional or official
sense in which the phrase had been sometimes used in
Jewish circles to designate the king, or, perhaps, the Messiah,[5] but rather in a metaphysical sense. He was " the only
begotten of the Father, full of grace and truth." [6]

The general idea of ascribing a kind of personal existence to the creative and revealing Word of God was no in-
vention of the early church. It lay at hand, although in
many variant forms, in Jewish Wisdom, Stoic philosophy,
and in whatever lies back of the Hermetic Gnosis. The
contribution of the church lay in the identifying of this
divine Word with Jesus. For this identification meant a
radical redefinition of the whole idea of the Word, as that
idea may have been known by members of the Christian
community. It is frequently debated whether the sources
of the early Christian conception of the Logos were predominantly Jewish or Hellenistic. The evidence on the
whole seems to point toward Hellenism.[7] I suggest, however, that the faith that *Jesus* was the Logos must have provided the decisive content for the Christian conception,
no matter from what sources the formal idea was derived.

But this is somewhat by the way. Our real point here
is that for many at the end of the first century Jesus, who
had walked the earth, was in a real sense God himself, in-
carnate in human form and manifesting his glory in great
supernatural acts. The divine Son of God had become
man, but without ceasing to be divine. Jesus of Nazareth

[5] The messianic reference is disputed by many. See Dalman, *The
Words of Jesus*, pp. 268 ff.; W. Manson, *Jesus the Messiah* (London: Hodder
& Stoughton, 1943), pp. 105 f.; A. E. J. Rawlinson, *The New Testament
Doctrine of Christ* (London: Longmans, Green & Co., 1926), pp. 251 ff.
Passages in dispute are such as II Sam. 7:14; Ps. 2:14; II Esdras 13:32.

[6] John 1:14.

[7] A strong defense of the view that the Johannine Logos idea was
derived largely from Hebraic-Jewish sources is made by R. H. Strachan,
The Historic Jesus in the New Testament (London: Student Christian
Movement Press, 1931), pp. 128 ff.

was in every important respect what he had been before the creation of the world, and was aware of himself as being such. This general view finds its fullest and clearest New Testament expression in the Fourth Gospel, as I have said, and in the First Epistle of John; [8] and the ways in which it was elaborated and defined in the great creedal discussions which culminated in the Chalcedonian formula are familiar.

Thus the process of theological interpretation of Jesus which began with what may be called adoptionism (a man become Lord) ended in a full-fledged incarnationism (God become man), according to which Jesus was not a man at all in any ordinary sense: he was the eternal Son of God made flesh and dwelling among us so that we beheld his glory. But if the beginning and end points of this development are clearly indicated in the most primitive strata of Acts and in the Fourth Gospel, the course it followed in the meantime is less clear.

A common view of how adoptionism became incarnationism is that the moment of "adoption," which was originally the resurrection, was, as the early communities reflected on the meaning of Jesus, moved forward into the historical life, and there pushed to an earlier and earlier point — from transfiguration, to baptism, to birth — until finally it was pushed out of the earthly life entirely and Jesus was conceived of as having been the Son of God before his birth. This view can be plausibly defended. It is clear

[8] My friend, Ernest C. Colwell, argues very persuasively in *John Defends the Gospel* (Chicago: Willett, Clark & Co., 1936), pp. 127 ff., that the author of the Fourth Gospel does not characteristically think in terms of the Logos. He uses the term only once, and that in what appears to be an adaptation of a Gnostic hymn. But whether he found the term congenial or not, there can be no doubt that he thought of Jesus as being the incarnation of a pre-existent divine being, who enjoyed a uniquely intimate intercourse with God and could supremely reveal him. Since I am not venturing to discuss here the origins and precise character of the Johannine Christology, this is enough for our purpose.

that theological interest in Jesus' earthly life began with the death and resurrection and moved backward. The earliest gospel preaching was dominated by these two events — or this one twofold event — as the quotation from Peter's sermon reminds us. But Mark, twenty-five years or so later, although he devotes half his space to the passion and events which immediately led up to it, gives also a summary account of Jesus' earlier career, beginning with his baptism — a career laden with supernatural significance. Matthew opens with the miraculous birth; and Luke makes an even earlier beginning, with the miraculous birth of John the Baptist, the forerunner of Jesus. In none of these Gospels does the doctrine of pre-existence clearly appear. When we notice, then, that the Fourth Gospel begins not with the baptism and birth, but with the eternal Logos, who " was in the beginning with God," it is not unnatural to decide that belief in the pre-existence of Jesus was the culmination of a process of exalting the earthly career which began with the fact of the resurrection and moved backward step by step till not only the whole of the earthly life was included but a divine pre-existence was affirmed as well.

The principal difficulty with this reconstruction is that it cannot easily accommodate the position of Paul. For Paul, while he takes the pre-existence for granted, evidently shares the "adoptionist" view of the significance of the resurrection. In large part because of this fact, but not without some warrant in the Gospels, I am inclined toward the view that belief in the pre-existence of Jesus did not follow, but rather preceded, the gradual exaltation of the earthly life; that the tendency toward a more and more supernaturalistic understanding of Jesus' earthly life, which can be seen operating from Gospel to Gospel and especially from the Synoptic Gospels to the Fourth, was created directly not by the resurrection faith but by belief in the pre-existent Christ. Reflection upon the resurrection led to the idea of pre-existence, and reflection upon the pre-existence led to the gradual supernaturalizing of Jesus' whole career. I believe that this development can be traced with some assurance, and a large part of the remainder of this lecture will be devoted to tracing it.

We start, as I said, with the position of Paul. That apostle begins his letter to the Romans with these words:

Paul, a servant of Jesus Christ, called to be an apostle, separated unto the gospel of God . . . concerning his Son, Jesus Christ our Lord, which was made of the seed of David according to the flesh and declared to be ["designated" and "installed as" are other ways of rendering the Greek term here] the Son of God with power according to the Spirit of holiness by the resurrection from the dead.

This statement is altogether in line with the words quoted from Acts as representative of the primitive view: "God hath made this same Jesus both Lord and Christ." In each case a son of man in the ordinary sense is spoken of as becoming the Son of God in a unique sense. So true is this of Paul's statement that interpreters have often said that the Roman church must have been "adoptionist" in its Christology and that Paul is expressing himself in language more congenial to its views than to his own. But this is an explanation to be accepted only as a last resort. One must begin by assuming that the words fairly represent Paul's own thought.

And indeed, so far as belief in the radical significance of the resurrection is concerned, there is more than enough to support this assumption. The letters of Paul contain not a single passage which associates any of the glory of the risen Son of God with the historical life of Jesus. Paul apparently knows of no transfiguration, of no signs and wonders. The glory breaks only at the resurrection. It was then that the human Jesus became the divine Lord. It was then that " God gave him the name that is above every name." The whole case for the saviorhood of Jesus stands or falls with the resurrection: " If Christ did not rise, then is your faith vain." [9] In fact, it is clear that Paul thought of Jesus' earthly life as having been more than ordinarily humble, and even shameful. Unless the reference to his having been a descendant of David can be regarded as an exception, Paul never alludes specifically to the earthly life except under some aspect of humiliation: " he took the nature of a slave "; " he became obedient to death, even the death of the cross "; " he was rich but for our sakes he became poor "; " he was born under the law "; " he who knew no sin became sin for us "; " he did not please himself." [10] Only at the resurrection did Jesus become Lord and Christ. This, as we have seen and as we would have expected, was undoubtedly the faith of the primitive church, and there is every reason to believe that Paul shared it. The quoted passage in Romans does not stand alone.

But although for Paul the remembered simplicity and lowliness of the historical life of Jesus have not been qualified at all (much less interpreted almost completely away, as in the Fourth Gospel), nevertheless he fully believes in Jesus' pre-existence. This appears clearly enough in the very letter whose opening words have been interpreted as pointing toward " adoptionism "; as, for example, when Paul speaks of God as " sending his own Son." [11] " He that

[9] I Cor. 15:14.
[10] Phil. 2:5 ff.; II Cor. 8:9; Gal. 4:4; II Cor. 5:21; Rom. 15:3.
[11] Rom. 8:3.

spared not his own Son but delivered him up for us all " [12]
points in the same direction.   In Galatians Paul is even
more explicit: " When the fulness of time came, God sent
forth his Son, born of a woman, born under the law." [13]
The pre-existent glory is brought into connection with the
remembered facts of Jesus' life in such passages as those
quoted in the preceding paragraph, of which II Corinthians 8:9 is typical: " Ye know the grace of our Lord Jesus
Christ, that, though he was rich, yet for our sakes he became
poor."   And in Philippians 2:6 ff. Paul brings all three
elements — pre-existent godhood, historical manhood, and
final exaltation — into one great picture:

> He possessed the nature of God, but he did not look upon
> equality with God as something to be violently seized, but he
> emptied himself and took the nature of a slave . . . and was
> obedient to death, even the death of the cross.   That is why God
> has exalted him and has given him a name that is above every
> name, that at the name of Jesus every knee should bow, in
> heaven, on earth and under the earth, and every tongue confess
> that Jesus Christ is Lord to the glory of God the Father.

This passage makes quite clear that Paul was able to hold
closely together a belief in the divine pre-existence of Jesus
and a recognition of the lowly and unqualified humanity
of the earthly life.   The resurrection stands in the same
stark contrast with the preceding phase as it did in the experience of Jesus' first disciples and as it did also in the
primitive " adoptionism," which was hardly more than a
transcript of that experience.   One gathers from the Philippians passage, as well as from such sentences as that
quoted from II Corinthians, that far from being embar-
rassed by the normality of the earthly life, Paul saw in it
a sign of how much Christ had been willing to sacrifice on
our behalf.   He loved us enough to lay aside his deity and

[12] Rom. 8:32.   [13] Gal. 4:4.

become a man, subject to all the limitations, weaknesses and frustrations which are man's lot. To deny the full reality of Jesus' humanity under every aspect of limitation would have seemed to Paul not only to fly in the face of the clearly remembered and indisputable facts of Jesus' life, but also to deny the full theological significance of that event. The " having the nature of God " had no importance apart from the " emptying " of self. If Christ had not become " very man," it did not much matter what he had been.

It appears then that for Paul at least belief in the pre-existence of Christ was not the result of a progressive exaltation of the earthly life. That process of exaltation had not begun. The first act as well as the third of the great drama takes place " in the heavenlies," but the second takes place upon the earth and partakes fully of the character of the earthly. The doctrine of pre-existence was the first, not the last, consequence of reflection upon the question: " Who *was* this person whom we knew as friend and teacher and whom we now know as Savior and Lord? "

But was Paul alone in this, or did he stand perhaps with only a small group within the church of the pre-Gospel period, that is, before 65 A.D.? I am persuaded that he was not alone, that his position on this matter was generally held among the non-Palestinian Gentile churches, perhaps among all the churches. The chief ground for this view is the manner in which Paul alludes to the pre-existence. He never does so with any apparent consciousness of having to prove a point. Every allusion is such as to suggest that Paul is dealing with an idea both familiar and indubitable. The pre-existence is taken for granted, needing no emphasis, elaboration, or proof. Paul's references to it are almost casual in manner, usually hints rather than explicit affirmations. In the Philippians passage, for example, Paul s really trying to teach a practical moral lesson: the believers at Philippi must not think primarily of themselves but must be modest and thoughtful of others. He remembers in that connection the divine person who, far from insisting on his rights, completely surrendered them for others; and before he knows it Paul is launched on the greatest christological statement he makes anywhere. But there is not the slightest sign that he is aware of doing more than reminding the Philippian believers of what they knew as well as he.

This casual character of the references to the pre-existence in Paul is even more obvious in the sentence I have several times quoted from II Corinthians: "For ye know the grace of our Lord Jesus Christ, that, though he was rich, yet for our sakes he became poor." Unless Paul had been able to take completely for granted an acquaintance with and acceptance of the idea of pre-existence, he could have had no expectation at all of being understood in this sentence. Apparently he did not even think of explaining in what sense Jesus was rich and then became poor; but that sense was, after all, a highly special sense, which would not occur to persons not fully initiated into the mysteries of Christ's pre-existence. The statement in Romans 15:3, " Christ did not please himself," is another case of the same kind.

The evidence of the Pauline letters suggests that in the years 40–60 A.D. the idea of the pre-existence of Christ was accepted not only by Paul himself but also by the churches generally. It thus followed directly upon reflection on the postresurrection glory of him whose earthly life was still distinctly remembered. It proved impossible to conclude that events ending in eternity had their beginning in time.[14]

---

[14] May it not be said that simple " adoptionism " (a man chosen and anointed to be the Christ) fits into the strict messianic pattern, but not

The belief in the pre-existence of Jesus was not the end result of the supernaturalizing of the earthly life (never complete except in Docetism), but the beginning of it. It was *because* Jesus was pre-existent that it became impossible to continue thinking of the earthly career as the normal human career it was at first remembered to have been.

The principal difficulty which this reconstruction, in turn, must face is the alleged " adoptionism " of the Synoptic Gospels, especially the Gospel of Mark. It is commonly said that there is no doctrine of pre-existence in Mark. If this is true, then one is forced to think of Paul's conception of Christ as having been, despite the data cited in the preceding paragraphs, largely his own and not representative of Christian reflection generally in his period. I gravely doubt that this view of Mark's Christology is true.

To be sure, Mark nowhere explicitly refers to the pre-existence. But one must not too quickly infer that he does not know it. We have seen that Paul alludes to this phase of Christ's reality only casually. He apparently takes it for granted as understood and only *happens* to mention it. I am convinced that the writer of Mark also took it for granted and happens *not* to mention it.

But does he altogether refrain from mentioning it? It is by no means clear that he does. I would not want to put too much weight on the passage, but it does not seem

into the more characteristically apocalyptic pattern? How, for example, could Jesus have been thought of as the Son of Man without the idea of pre-existence being at least implicit? According to Schweitzer and Otto, Jesus believed he *would become* the Son of Man; but this means that he would assume a personality which was *even then* already in existence (but see note 16, below). Pre-existence is essential in the Son of Man idea, and Jesus could hardly have been thought of as being the Son of Man (or an eschatological Redeemer, whatever terms were used) without the conception being present. It might not be recognized at first, but it was certain to emerge almost at once.

certain to me that Mark 1:38 is not making the sort of casual allusion to the pre-existence which we have noted in Paul. In the Authorized Version we read: " And he said unto them, Let us go into the next towns that I may preach there also: for therefore came I forth." There can be little question that the English translators thought of the verse as having the meaning I have suggested, and it seems probable to me that Mark did also; unquestionably most of his readers did.[15] Both Goodspeed and Moffatt render the last clause: " for that is why I came out here." If the words were actually spoken by Jesus, we can be far surer that something like that was *his* meaning than that it was the meaning Mark found in his words.

Perhaps a clearer reference to pre-existence is to be found in Mark 10:45, already cited: " The son of man came not to be ministered unto, but to minister, and to give his life a ransom for many." Would not this statement be almost certainly understood by Mark's first readers as a reference to Christ's coming into this world from the heavenly realm?

An even more likely allusion appears in Mark 12:35 ff., where Jesus is represented as saying:

How is it that the scribes say that the Messiah is the Son of David? David himself said by means of the Holy Spirit, The Lord said unto my Lord, Sit thou on my right hand till I make thine enemies the footstool of thy feet. David himself calls him Lord, and how can he be his son?

Certainly this passage can be most naturally interpreted on the assumption that Mark thinks of Jesus as being a pre-existent supernatural being, to whom David could address himself.[16]

---

15 Notice the meaning Luke finds in the verse: " therefore was I sent " (Luke 4:43).

16 One cannot press too hard here. The pre-existence of the Christ might be in " name " only. He is pre-existent in the sense that he is foreknown by God; he pre-exists in God's purpose. This kind of pre-

It may also be remarked that Mark's literary purpose would rule out the inclusion of too explicit an allusion to the pre-existence. The Gospel of Mark is in many ways quite unliterary, sometimes almost crude; its author was not one of the better Greek writers of the New Testament. But it has a strange power and was written by a man of unusual dramatic gifts. That Jesus was a supernatural person is clear to the reader from the very beginning, but this fact is represented as having been hidden from Jesus' contemporaries. The demons, because they had supernatural insight, were able to sense his true nature, and they cried out that he should spare them. But to only a few men was the secret revealed and to them only gradually. (Notice the secrecy which is likely to surround the miracles, especially the greatest of them.) The open references to the pre-existence which we find in the Fourth Gospel would not have suited Mark's purpose.

It has always seemed to me that light is thrown on Mark's failure to refer explicitly to the pre-existence at the beginning of his book by the way he chooses to end it. We have already observed that Mark ends with a finger pointing toward the risen and exalted Jesus, who does not himself appear. In the same way the book begins with a finger pointing toward the pre-existent Christ, but without that Christ's actually appearing. Quoting from Malachi, Mark

---

existence could be very real to the Hebrew-Jewish mind. This, Otto holds, is the only sense in which Enoch's "Son of Man" was pre-existent (*The Kingdom of God and the Son of Man*, pp. 214 f.). But on the assumption that the remark goes back to Jesus himself, it is much more likely that he had such a thought in his mind than that the author of Mark had when he reported the saying. Otto, interpreting Enoch, writes: "Enoch as Enoch was by no means pre-existent. The conception was rather this, that he, the man Enoch, became and was elevated to something which already existed hidden with God (as name or as reality), but which as such was not the already pre-existent Enoch himself." But here is a subtlety more credible, it seems to me, in the Jewish Apocalypse than in the Roman Gospel.

understands God through the prophet to be saying of John
and *to* Christ: " Behold I send my messenger before thy
face; he shall prepare thy way." Mark seeks to keep himself strictly to the earthly scene and to present only the
second act of the drama which began in heaven and ended
there. But his book both begins and ends in a manner
designed to make clear that what it contains is only the
middle episode of a vastly larger story. It ends with a
proclamation of the risen and exalted Jesus; it begins with
an allusion, only slightly less explicit, to the pre-existent
Christ. The baptism in Mark is not the moment when a
natural man becomes the supernatural Messiah. It is
the moment when an essentially supernatural person is
anointed for his messianic office — the moment perhaps
when he himself first becomes aware of the vocation which
it is laid upon him as a man to fulfill for Israel and all mankind. It is the moment of " installation " (cf. Romans
1:4) ; and Mark's conception of its significance conflicts
with the idea of the pre-existence as little as does Paul's
understanding of the significance of the resurrection.

It is interesting to notice in this connection the appearances in the tradition of the divine pronouncement upon
Jesus, " This is my beloved son," or " Thou art my beloved
son " — which is a quotation, more or less exact, from the
second Psalm. This pronouncement in somewhat variant
forms appears in connection with three events in the tradition: the baptism, the transfiguration, and the resurrection.[17] If we may assume (as it seems to me we must
assume) that the quotation was first used at one of these
points only and was afterward extended to the others, we
can scarcely doubt that this point was the resurrection. So
used, the quotation would correspond exactly with Paul's
statement, " declared to be the Son of God with power

---

[17] Mark 1:11 and parallels; Mark 9:7 and parallels; Acts 13:33.

through the resurrection from the dead." As the tradition developed and the community moved farther and farther away from eyewitness knowledge, the moment of this declaration, or designation, or installation, was moved farther and farther into the earthly life, being associated first with the transfiguration (which was itself probably an original resurrection appearance moved forward into the earthly life [18]) and later with the baptism, while in Matthew, Jesus is represented as having been, in effect, " designated Son of God with power " from the moment of his birth, and, in Luke, even before. But at none of these stages are we justified in supposing that anything more than the *designation* of Jesus as Christ and Son of God was involved. There is more than sufficient reason to affirm that Mark, Matthew and Luke, as well as Paul, took for granted the pre-existence of Jesus.[19]

[18] It is interesting to observe how Mark likes to describe events in proleptic fashion. There is no resurrection appearance in Mark, but here in the transfiguration scene is an unmistakable anticipation of such an appearance. The passion story ends with some women coming to anoint the body of Jesus and being unable to do so because the body is gone, but the passion story begins (14:1) with the account of a woman breaking on him " an alabaster box of ointment, very precious," while Jesus says of her, " She has anointed me beforehand for my burial." Is it too fanciful to suggest that Mark includes in his moving, tragic account of the passion the apparently whimsical story about the young man who was seized at the moment of Jesus' arrest and ran away naked, leaving a linen cloth in the hands of his captors (14:51 f.) — is it too fanciful to suggest that this item is included because Mark, or some early community, saw in it an anticipation of the empty tomb, with which this Gospel culminates? Notice that in Mark 15:46 Jesus' body is wrapped in a linen cloth. In the resurrection story in the Fourth Gospel, Peter and John find the body gone but see the linen cloths lying in the sepulcher. In the Acts of Pilate we read: " And when they were come to the place they stripped him of his garments and girt him with a linen cloth. . . . And Joseph took it [Jesus' body] down and wrapped it in a clean linen cloth." Jerome in *Of Illustrious Men*, 2, quotes from " the Gospel according to the Hebrews ": " Now the Lord [after the resurrection], when he had given the linen cloth unto the servant of the priest, appeared unto James . . ." See also Gospel of Peter 6:24.

[19] We have made no effort to include all of the New Testament in this survey, but a word or two at least must be said about the Christology of

In this matter then, as in so many others, the line of theological development moves from the most primitive church, through Paul, through Mark, to John. In Paul the pre-existent Son of God surrenders his divine nature and status to become a man, even a slave, for man's sake; in Mark he becomes a man, but without surrendering so completely his divine powers — they are only held in abeyance for a while; in John the Word becomes flesh without any significant surrender of divine prerogatives. In Paul the pre-existent glory is forsaken for the humble human life; in Mark it is hidden, though it is too brilliant to be hidden altogether; in John the glory is manifest for all except the most perversely blind to behold.

---

the Epistle to the Hebrews, which is probably to be dated in the last decade of the first century. One has only to read the first chapter of the epistle (really, only the first three verses of that chapter) to see clearly not only that the author has a firm belief in the pre-existence of Christ (and takes such a belief for granted in his readers) but also that he thinks of the pre-existence in the most exalted terms. Christ was the "Son," "appointed heir of all things," "by whom also God made the worlds," "being the brightness of his glory and the express image of his person," "upholding all things by the word of his power." Here obviously we have a "Logos" or "Wisdom" Christology (cf. Wisdom 7:25 ff.) , which in the New Testament is matched only in the Fourth Gospel. But the epistle is quite unlike the Fourth Gospel in the emphasis it places upon the reality of the humanity. To be sure, the Fourth Gospel insists strongly upon the formal fact; there is an emphatic repudiation of Docetism; not even Paul affirms the humanity so bluntly and unequivocally as does the Fourth Gospel in the sentence, "The Word was made flesh" (John 1:14) . But although this Gospel emphasizes the formal fact, one does not sense in it much feeling for the concrete reality. John would not have said (as Hebrews does) that Jesus "was touched with the feeling of our infirmities," that "he was tempted in all points like as we are," that "he offered up prayers and supplications with strong crying and tears unto him that was able to save him from death," that "though he was a Son, yet learned he obedience through the things that he suffered" (Heb. 4:15; 5:7 f.). In his recognition of the deep significance of the human sufferings of Jesus the writer to the Hebrews stands nearer to Paul than to John. See the short statement on the Christology of Hebrews, particularly helpful to me in the note I have just written, in Vincent Taylor, *The Atonement in New Testament Teaching* (London: Epworth Press, 1940) , pp. 166 ff.; and more extended discussions in Strachan, *The Historic Jesus in the New Testament*, pp. 74 ff., and in H. L. MacNeill, *The Christology of the Epistle to the Hebrews* (Chicago: University of Chicago Press, 1914) .

The particular way in which Paul (and this is even more true of Mark) conceived of Jesus' pre-existence is less clear than the pre-existence itself. There is one passage in Paul's letters which indicates a view virtually identical with the Logos Christology we have mentioned as characteristic of the Fourth Gospel. This is Colossians 1:15 ff.:

Who [Jesus] is the image of the invisible God; the firstborn of all creation; for in him all things were created, in the heavens and upon the earth, visible and invisible, whether thrones, or dominions, or principalities, or powers; all things have been created by him and for him; and he himself is before all things and in him all things consist.

No passage in the nine letters of Paul is more open to suspicion than this one, and it is precarious to base any argument upon it.[20] The only other statement in Paul's writings which comes even near to expressing the same christological view is I Corinthians 8:6: " To us there is one God, the Father, from whom are all things, and we unto him; and one Lord, Jesus Christ, through whom are all things and we through him." But this sentence, even if its authenticity be regarded as certain, can be interpreted otherwise than as a reference to the creative Logos or Wisdom. This can be said, with even greater assurance, of

[20] As was intimated early in this book, Colossians is one of the less certainly established letters of Paul. The more radical critics have always rejected it and even the more conservative have been compelled to question its authenticity. For myself, I feel sure (for reasons suggested in the article, " Philemon and the Authenticity of Colossians," *Journal of Religion*, XVIII [1938], 144 ff.) that Paul wrote a letter to the church at Colossae which corresponds generally with the document we have; but I am strongly inclined to believe that the letter has undergone considerable interpolation. The work of H. J. Holtzmann, *Kritik der Epheser und Kolosserbriefe auf Grund einer Analyse ihres Verwandtschaftsverhältnisses* (Leipzig, 1872), especially as it touches the question of the authenticity of Colossians, has probably been too quickly dismissed, and the more plausible suggestions of C. R. Bowen (" The Original Form of Paul's Letter to the Colossians," *Journal of Biblical Literature*, XLIII [1924], pp. 177 ff.) have received too little attention.

I Corinthians 1:24, where Christ is described as " the power and the wisdom of God."

The most explicit reference to the pre-existence in Paul, that in Philippians 2:5 ff., leaves the question of precise character open. The important thing was that a divine being — one who had " the nature of God " — abased himself. It is hard to resist the conclusion that Paul is thinking of this divine person in contrast to the mythological Lucifer (see Isaiah 14:12 ff.) , who *did* seek to seize " by robbery " equality with God and in consequence was thrown out of heaven. Jesus, on the contrary, far from grasping at higher powers, willingly divested himself of those which he possessed and voluntarily left heaven to suffer as a man upon the earth.[21]   If this contrast is in Paul's mind, the myth of

---

[21] It has been claimed by many that Paul thought of Christ as having been a man in his pre-existence. Pfleiderer, for example, writes: " We cannot without violence reject the idea that the human person who had his origin from heaven had also pre-existed in heaven as man, as *the same subject* and in *the same form of existence*, as that in which he continues to live in heaven as the exalted one " (*Paulinism* [London: Williams & Norgate, 1891], I, 139) . In that case the incarnation involved merely the taking of flesh in the narrow sense of the word, since Christ would have been man already. (On this whole question of a pre-existent Man, see the book to which reference has already been made in connection with the idea of the Son of Man: Kraeling, *Anthropos and Son of Man*.)   A parallel to Paul's conception of the pre-existence is found by some in Philo's Platonic conception of the ideal Man (see *De Leg. Alleg.* I, 12, 13, and *De Mundi Opif.* 46) . Philo interpreted the two accounts of the creation of man in Gen. 1 and 2 as representing two separate creations: first, the ideal, archetypal Man in heaven, and then, Adam, the actual historical man. It is sometimes argued that Paul has some such conception in his mind, and that he thinks of Jesus as being the actualization of the original, perfect, spiritual man. Paul's idea that Christ heads a new spiritual humanity just as Adam heads natural humanity (I Cor. 15:45 ff.; Rom. 5:12 ff.) is cited in support of this understanding (see below, pp. 120 ff.).

But, to mention one important point of difference, in Paul the spiritual man is the second man, whereas in Philo he is the original man. In Paul, Adam has been the head of the old humanity; Christ *by his resurrection* becomes the head of the new humanity.

But not only is it true that I Cor. 15:45-49 does not (to say the least) require anything resembling the Philonic view; it should also be recognized that the Philippians passage rather decidedly contradicts it. There will be some to deny this. Everything turns on Paul's meaning in the

the rebellious angels may throw some light on the way in which he thought of Jesus' pre-existence. Christ's original nature and status could not have been altogether incommensurable with theirs. With greater certainty we can say that according to the Philippians passage Paul does not think of the risen Jesus as merely resuming a place he had temporarily resigned. He is exalted to a new title and office, different from — and, one would gather, higher than — those he had held in his pre-existence. Now he has been given the name and status of *Kyrios* [22] and has become worthy of a worship far beyond any he received before his abasement and consequent exaltation. This view is not easily compatible with a high Logos Christology.

As to the manner in which the nature and status of the *risen* Jesus were conceived in the early church, both by Paul and by others, we can feel greater assurance. He was "Lord and Christ." He was the Lord — that is, he was the center and head of the church, to whom obedience and worship were given and who as the Spirit was constantly present within the fellowship and with those who belonged

phrase, "the form of God." I have taken it to mean "the nature of God," the "category of God." But some see in μορφή here a translation of an Aramaic original which meant simply "image" or "likeness." In that case, Paul is here referring to Christ as having been (like Adam) in the image of God, but (unlike Adam) as having lacked or renounced any ambition to be "like God" (Gen. 3:5); on the contrary, he emptied himself and took on the aspect of a slave. It seems to me more likely, however, that the myth of the rebellious angels is in Paul's mind rather than that of Adam's disobedience. Not only is the phrase, "the form of God," set over against the corresponding phrase, "the form of a slave," in such a way as to suggest an opposition of the most radical and absolute kind, but the term "robbery" in this passage suggests the analogy of the Lucifer myth. Translations usually fail to convey the real force of this term because, except in the light of the myth, it has no particular relevance here.

[22] Is this the "equality with God," referred to earlier in this passage? Κύριος was God's own name, according to the Septuagint.

to it. He was also the Christ — that is, he was the man, now exalted to God's right hand, who would shortly come in glorious power to judge the world and inaugurate the new age.

It is really impossible to harmonize these two conceptions: Christ the Spirit and Christ the expected eschatological Judge and Savior. But it is also impossible to eliminate either strain from early Christian thinking about Jesus. It is not difficult to show that Paul, for example, does not think of Jesus only as the spiritual Lord (he expects him to come from heaven, when the trumpet sounds, to judge the world and save the faithful: " We shall be caught up to meet him in the air " [23]) ; but it is also not difficult to show that he does not think of him only as an eschatological Messiah (he can say, " I live, and yet not I, but Christ liveth in me " [24]) . Here is a logical contradiction in Paul's thought, and in early Christian thought generally, which we can only accept. By the time of the Fourth Gospel, at least in the circles for which it speaks, the eschatological functions of the Messiah were thought of as having been discharged during Jesus' earthly life (judgment and salvation had already come) ; Christ is *now* the Spirit and the Lord. It was from the first perhaps inevitable that Jesus' lordship, rather than his messiahship, should dominate the church's Christology, because his lordship was a matter of present knowledge, while his messiahship was a matter largely of expectation and hope. But at the beginning the two conceptions, logically incompatible, were held closely together.

This was possible partly because the messianic hope was so vivid and was so intimately related to the present experiences of the community. For the eschatological hope was not a hope only; the return of Jesus as Inaugurator of

<hr/>

[23] I Thes. 4:17.　　　　[24] Gal. 2:20.

the age to come would be but the culmination of an event which had *already begun* and was now far advanced, the eschatological event with which history was ending.[25]   The presence of the Lord, the Spirit, in the church was more than the promise of a future kingdom; it was the kingdom already beginning to come.   Members of the community had received the Spirit as an " earnest," an advance installment, of the new age they were soon fully to inherit.   The church was the present core or seed of that new age, and the new life was already available to those who by penitence and faith would enter her open gates.

We frequently search for some previously existing pattern of messianic expectation to which the thought of the early church about Jesus conformed.   No such pattern can be found.   The strictly messianic conception applies only to the extent that a man is conceived of as being (or as having been made) Christ. But the pre-existence of this man, his death and resurrection, and the expectation of his final coming from heaven do not belong to this conception. The " Son of Man " pattern applies more closely, but it does not make room for the man Jesus (unless Otto's interpretation of Enoch is accepted), and in any case not for his death. One is forced to recognize that the early church,

[25] It is obvious that such an interpretation of history could maintain itself only so long as the earthly career was vividly remembered and the " second coming " was vividly expected. As time passed, and the earthly life faded into the past and the second advent into the remoter future, one of two alternatives was open: Either the whole saving event could be put in the past, in close conjunction with the earthly career, or else it could be entirely postponed to the future, in close connection with the *Parousia*. The first of these alternatives is exemplified in the Fourth Gospel, where the meaning of the return of Christ is all but exhausted in the coming of the Spirit upon the church and where the whole content of redemption is involved in the incarnation, which is a past event — present and future only in the sense that it is perpetuated in the life of the community. Less consistently the second alternative is exemplified in the book of Revelation, where the whole process of salvation tends to be associated with the future advent of the Messiah, although the expiatory significance of Christ's death is constantly in the author's mind.

out of its own experience and faith, created its own christological pattern, using elements from both of these conceptions and from other sources also; as, for example, from the
Suffering Servant passages of Isaiah. " Messiah " was the
highest title the Jew knew how to bestow upon a man. For
that reason it was inevitable that it should be bestowed
upon Jesus. The meaning it came to have, as thus bestowed, was determined not by any prior, formal idea of
the office, but by the church's memory of Jesus the man,
by its knowledge of him as Lord, and by its faith that he
would soon be manifested before all the world as Judge
and Savior.

At the beginning of these lectures I said that a study of
the meaning of Jesus in the early church would involve a
study of both life and dogma, of both Christ and Christology, and that there could be no doubt that life is more important than dogma, Christ than Christology. This is true,
but it is also true that we cannot understand the life of the
early church if we neglect its dogma, or the meaning of
Christ for it if we dismiss its Christology. We cannot know
him, as he was and is, if we disregard the ways in which the
early church sought to explain him. In trying to *explain*
the real meaning of Jesus, the early church did something
more important than explaining it — they succeeded in
conveying it. The Christology of the early church is most
important because it leads us to the Christ of the early
church. We could not know what Jesus really meant if
they had not tried to explain why he meant so much.

Lecture VI

SO FAR, in this discussion of early Christian attempts to interpret Jesus, we have been considering the question of the *nature* of Christ; we must now ask about the *work* of Christ. From our examination of the primitive church's answer to the question, " Who *was* this Jesus? " we now turn to the answer it gave to the question, " What did he do for man? " I shall depart somewhat from the method of preceding lectures and shall attempt little more than to present the position of Paul, whom this question so constantly engaged. I shall do this not because there are not significant differences in the way various New Testament writers interpreted what Christ had accomplished, but because there will not be opportunity to present at all adequately each of these divergent views; and if one must choose, Paul's view is by every criterion the most important. In general it may be said that the same line of development from the most primitive strata in Acts, to Paul, to John can be traced in early Christian thinking about the work of Christ as we have noted in the primitive church's reflection upon his nature. References to these sources, and others, will occasionally be made; but the focus of attention, even more than in the preceding lecture, will be upon Paul.[1]

At the very outset it is well to remember that the question, " What did he do? " is not to be taken as meaning, " Did he

[1] For a more adequate discussion of New Testament teaching in its several parts see Taylor, *The Atonement in New Testament Teaching;* or the earlier work of James Denney, *The Death of Christ* (New York: A. C. Armstrong & Son, 1903).

do anything very important?" The supreme significance of what Jesus had accomplished was never in debate. The fact of the divine saviorhood of Jesus was a matter of experience, as I sought to emphasize in the first two sections of this book. The first believers knew they had been "saved"— that is, they knew they had been forgiven and reconciled to God; that they had been incorporated into a new and divine community and had received a new and divine life. They knew also that this had happened "through Christ." The question was: How and why was this true? In just what way did Jesus accomplish all of this for them? How were they to *understand* the saviorhood of Jesus?

The very term "saviorhood" suggests man's need of salvation, and any discussion of soteriology must begin with anthropology, in the sense in which the theologians use that term. Paul's whole theology begins with a diagnosis of the human situation, and the truth and pertinence of that theology depend almost entirely upon whether that diagnosis is sound. If we find true Paul's view of man and his condition, we shall probably both understand and find acceptable everything else of a fundamental sort that Paul has to say. If, on the other hand, we regard Paul's answer to the question, "What is man?" as a false answer, all that he says besides will be likely to seem to us either meaningless or incredible.

Paul's answer begins where any Jewish answer to this question must have begun: with an affirmation of man's creaturehood. God created man, and created him in his own image. Thus God set him above the beasts of the field and crowned him with glory and honor. The breath of the divine was in him and the law of God was written in his heart. Man was thus the child of God, delighting to do his will. There was peace within himself, and between himself and his whole environment, because there was peace between himself and God.

But this original goodness and beatitude did not continue. Man became separated from God, estranged from his Creator. This estrangement occurred not because God turned away from man, but because sin made its way into human life and established itself there, distorting what God had made, destroying the original balance and harmony of creation, and turning man's heart from obedience and fellowship to transgression and rebellion.

I hardly need to say that this understanding of man was not original with Paul; he derived it from the Judaism in which he was reared and which he never consciously forsook. The stories of the creation and the fall of man in the first three chapters of Genesis are together nothing other than a primitive statement of that same understanding. They purport to be accounts of some events which happened in the remote past, and, of course, were intended and for the most part received as such, quite literally and naïvely. But what the stories are really concerned to do is to set forth an answer to the question, "What is man?" and they are false only if that answer is untrue.[2] Man, the creation story says, has capacities and powers which raise him far above the rest of creation and make him capable of fellowship and of conscious cooperation with his Creator; but, says the story of the fall, not only is he actually falling short of the glory of God for which he was created, but his very spiritual capacities have been corrupted and perverted, so that whereas on the one hand he is infinitely

[2] I am aware that biblical scholars sometimes deny that this is in any sense the intention of these myths. I can only say that in my opinion such scholars are too cautious on this point. But whatever may have been the original meaning, there is plenty of evidence that in Paul's time the myths were understood as having decisive bearing upon human nature and the course of history. See H. St. J. Thackeray, *The Relation of St. Paul to Contemporary Jewish Thought* (London: Macmillan Co., 1900), chap. 2.

bove the beasts, on the other he is infinitely beneath them.

Man is not an animal, belonging simply to the natural
world; he shares the image of God. But the position is
more complicated still: this image of God is, as it were, distorted.[3] What more natural than that such an understanding of the character of " existent human nature " should
express itself in the belief that man was created in God's
likeness but was overtaken by a vast moral catastrophe
which irremediably marred that likeness, set man at odds
with his Creator and with himself, and not only thwarted
the realization of his true nature but also hopelessly perverted it, turning what was created for the service of God to
the service of demons? This is the understanding of human
nature which is presupposed in all the profounder parts of
the New Testament. It was undoubtedly Paul's understanding.

The cause of man's failure has already been identified as
sin; and it is important to understand as clearly as possible
what this term meant for Paul. Here again a reference to
the Old Testament is appropriate. Of the many terms used
for sin in the Old Testament some suggest a failure to " hit
the mark " or to conform to some objective standard of con-
duct, and others suggest an attitude of disloyalty to a person. In the prophets, in whom Old Testament religion
has its highest and most authentic expression, the second of
these two senses is much the more important. Sin is rebel-

[3] John Baillie, in *Our Knowledge of God* (New York: Charles Scribner's Sons, 1939) , p. 23, writes: " The doctrine of the *imago dei* has its basis
in the fact that our existent human nature presents itself to us, not as a
simply bad thing, but as *a good thing spoiled.*" No one has written with
greater acuteness on this matter than Reinhold Niebuhr, and I am greatly
indebted to him, here and elsewhere. See his *An Interpretation of Christian Ethics* (New York: Harper & Brothers, 1935) , especially chap. 3,
and *The Nature and Destiny of Man* (New York: Charles Scribner's Sons,
1943) , Vol. I.

lion against God, or at least unfaithfulness toward him
Social injustice within Israel, for example, which calle
forth the sternest protests of the prophets, was not merel
a violation of the command of Yahweh: it was sin agains
Yahweh himself, who had identified himself with th
people he had chosen.   On this issue there is no doubt tha
Paul stood with the prophets, as against more legalisti
ways of interpreting the will of God.   But the term " sin
has for him another, deeper meaning.   According to th
meaning, sin is not merely the act or condition of rebellio
against God, but is the very Spirit of rebellion itself.   Th
act of disloyalty (although it may be called " sin ") is, mor
profoundly, the consequence of sin: sin makes us do wron
and keeps us from doing right.   Sin itself is a demoni
power, alien to man in his true nature, which has got er
trance into human life and has brought it into subjectior

This understanding of man as being actually (althoug
not essentially) the slave of sin is expressed again and agai
in Paul's writings, never more poignantly than in the fina
sentences of Romans, chapter 7:

The law is spiritual, but I am carnal, sold into slavery t
sin. . . . I do not do the things I want to do; I do things tha
I hate. . . . It is no longer I who do these things; it is sir
which possesses me. . . . To will the good is possible for me bu
to do it is impossible.   I do not do the good I want to do
I do the evil I do not want to do. . . . It is not I who am actin
thus, it is sin which has possession of me.

This sin has possession of the individual because the in
dividual is part of the race.   Sin for Paul (as for many bil
lical writers) is a massive social or racial fact.   Not simpl
every man separately, but man — human nature — has be
come infected and corrupted by sin.   To be human is t
be a sinner: not, I repeat, that man or any part of him i
constitutionally evil — there is no ultimate dualism i

Paul any more than in orthodox Judaism. But racial man, as he is actually found, is in the grip of sin, and no individual can free himself from that bondage. There is, to use a phrase of C. H. Dodd, a " fundamental wrongness " in human life, in which every living man is inescapably involved; a " reprobate character," a tendency toward evil, which no man can successfully resist. This reprobate character is known not only through an individual's own experience with himself as he struggles with impulses too strong for his own strength to overcome, but also through his observation of the world about him, a world in which evil and its works are so terribly apparent, and in whose operations he is so inextricably involved.

Sin is thus a demonic power which through Adam's disobedience gained access to man's interior life. Taking up its seat in man's flesh,[4] it has upset the primeval balance of God's creation and reduced man's diviner part to an abject slavery. Man is the slave of sin, and disorder and death are the lot of all mankind.

This death is not so much an arbitrary penalty as an inevitable consequence. " The *wages* of sin is death." Sin *works itself out* in decay and destruction. Paul's term for this destruction is " the Wrath " or, occasionally, " the Wrath of God." Dodd points out that the relative infrequency of the latter, more personal, form of the phrase, together with the fact that Paul never makes God the subject of the verb " to be angry," should put us on guard against supposing that he is thinking of any personal attitude of God toward men when he speaks of " the Wrath." [5] He

[4] Paul is no doubt influenced here by Hellenistic dualism between flesh and spirit, although it is to be noted that he does not regard flesh as being essentially evil. Still, it is the seat of sin and is undoubtedly thought of as having been especially corrupted by it.

[5] C. H. Dodd, *The Epistle of Paul to the Romans* (New York and London: Harper & Brothers, 1932) , pp. 20 ff.

is speaking primarily not of an attitude at all, but of an event — the corruption and death whose working he feels within his own body (" Who will deliver me from this body of death? ") and sees horribly revealed in the perversions and degradations around him:

> So God abandoned them, with their heart's cravings, to impurity, and let them degrade their own bodies. For they had exchanged the truth of God for what was false, and worshipped and served what he had created, instead of the Creator, who is blessed forever! Amen! That is why God has abandoned them to degrading passions. . . . They revel in every kind of wrongdoing, wickedness, greed, and depravity. They are full of envy, murder, quarrelling, deceit, and ill-nature. They are gossips, slanderers, abhorrent to God, insolent, overbearing, boastful, ingenious in evil, undutiful, conscienceless, treacherous, unloving, and unpitying. They know God's decree that those who act in this way deserve to die, yet they not only do it, but applaud any who do.[6]

But although Dodd's emphasis upon the objective character of " the Wrath " is justified, nevertheless it is clear from this very passage that Paul did not hesitate to ascribe to God responsibility for this judgment. It is God who has " abandoned " sinful men " to degrading passions " and it is God whose " decree that those who act in this way deserve to die " they have disregarded and flaunted. Thus although we must not suppose that he thought of God as being angry in the way men are angry, still Paul is aware that the divine righteousness has been outraged by man's sin. " The Wrath " is not merely the final issue of man's bondage (see Romans 6:16 ff.) ; it is also God's sentence upon man's guilt.

We confront here another of the many contradictions in Paul's thought: man is helpless in the grip of sin, but man

[6] Rom. 1:24–32. (E. J. Goodspeed's translation [*The Bible: An American Translation*] is used by permission of the University of Chicago Press.)

is responsible for sin. This contradiction cannot be re-
solved — but do the facts permit that it be avoided?
Again, the final test of the truth of Paul's view is not
whether it is logically consistent, but whether it answers
to the real human situation. Actually is it not true that
though we do know ourselves helpless to do God's perfect
will, helpless to resist successfully the temptations to pride
and selfishness which assail us in every area of our life and
at every level of moral endeavor, we nevertheless know that
we are guilty before God and that we should be guilty even
if we should make the maximum effort of which human
flesh is capable? We know ourselves actually to be amenable to a law of purity and love which our sinfulness will
forever keep us from fulfilling. No logically consistent
statement can cover and interpret this fact, but the fact is
unmistakable. And Paul's view of man's condition (and
in its essentials his is the central biblical view) cannot be
declared false, for all its mythical character, so long as it is
the only view of man which takes adequate account of this
inescapable reality of human experience: On the one hand,
I know that " it is not I who do these things but sin which
has possession of me "; but, on the other hand, I know that
I am responsible for these acts of sin and that I deserve to
die because of them.

Of both this bondage and this guilt the law, according to
Paul, makes us aware, and it was divinely designed and
given with that purpose. No problem confronting the
interpreter of Paul's thought is likely to seem so difficult
as how to understand his conception of the law. This is
true because, in all probability, the law proved an almost
insoluble problem for Paul himself. He was a good Jew
and as such could not think of questioning the divine
source and the authority of the law; and yet desperately
earnest attempts at obedience had convinced him of the

futility of expecting salvation through that means. Indeed, the law had served only to bring into vivid relief the
reality of his alienation from God and his bondage to the
power of sin. More than that, the commandments had
sometimes had the effect of stirring sinful impulses, which
were sleeping, into activity. Thus he can write:

> I had not known sin, but by the law; for I would not have
> known lust unless the law had said, Thou shalt not covet. But
> sin, taking occasion by the commandment, wrought in me all
> manner of sinful desire. For without the law sin was dead.
> For I was alive without the law once; but when the command-
> ment came, sin revived and I died. And the commandment,
> which was for life, I found to be for death. For sin taking
> occasion by the commandment deceived me, and by it slew
> me.[7]

In this way bondage to sin and bondage to the law —
utterly opposite though these two elements might seem to
be — could appear to Paul as one bondage. Without the
law there would have been no awareness of his slavery to
sin; and without sin, the law would not have appeared as
the hard taskmaster it was, since in that case he could easily
and naturally have given the required obedience. Thus,
in spite of its divine origin, Paul could think of the law
as one of the three great enemies from which man needs to
be delivered: " The sting of death is sin, and the strength
of sin is the law."[8]   " The law was a tutor to bring us to
Christ," Paul says on another occasion; [9] but he is not alluding to any gradual approach to Christ through obedience to
the law. He means that attempts to fulfill the law produce
the despair of self which must precede one's acceptance in
faith of salvation, which is not achieved by man's effort but
is bestowed in Christ by God's grace. The law stands as
a reminder of God's righteous will, but also of man's moral

[7] Rom. 7:7 ff.   [8] I Cor. 15:56.   [9] Gal. 3:24.

impotence and of his need of a redemption which only God can bring.

Paul's whole conception of man — his creation in God's own image with the law of God written in his heart, his losing battle with a demonic enemy, the shameful captivity in which he is now held and the doom of death which awaits him — this whole conception, as well as the despair of one who awakes to the realities for which the conception stands, is expressed in the words with which Paul ends what we know as the seventh chapter of Romans:

> I delight in the law of God after the inward man, but I find another law in my members, warring against the law of my mind and bringing me into captivity to the law of sin which is in my members. O wretched man that I am! Who will deliver me from this body of death!

This poignant cry is followed at once by the triumphant shout, " I thank God, through Jesus Christ our Lord "; just as Paul's reference to man's bondage to sin and death in I Corinthians 15:56, quoted a moment ago, is immediately followed by " Thanks be to God who giveth us the victory through our Lord Jesus Christ."   It was Paul's most certain, most intimate, and most central conviction that God has brought deliverance, and that he has done so through Christ: " What the law could not do because it was weak through the flesh, God did by sending his own son in the likeness of sinful flesh and for sin. He placed sin in the flesh under sentence of death." [10]   The law indeed, as we have seen, had not only been too weak to destroy sin in the flesh; it had actually stirred sin into activity. But God in Christ has broken the grip of sin and set us free — free from both its guilt and its power. In him both forgiveness and new life are made available for us.

But the question with which this lecture began still re-

[10] Rom. 8:1 f.

mains: How did Paul understand that this had been accomplished?

We have seen that Paul's understanding of the realities of the human situation apart from Christ could be expressed only in mythological terms, and the suggestion has been made that, in the nature of the case, this must be true, not for him only, but also for us, if our understanding is at all adequate or profound. This fact about Paul will prepare us to find that his interpretation of the " work " of Christ makes use of similar terms. Indeed, it may be said that whenever Paul speaks of what Christ accomplished (or of what God accomplished through him), his language is either mythical or metaphorical; and the distinction between myth and metaphor is not always easy to draw.

Paul nowhere gives a systematic statement of his views on this matter, but if one will read through his letters, carefully noting every reference to what Christ did for man, or what God did for man through him, one will discover the use, in some cases frequently recurring, of some five rather distinct images, which may be roughly indicated as follows:

1. Jesus paid a ransom on our behalf and thus secured our release from the slavery of sin.

2. He satisfied the requirements of the law for us; he paid a penalty we could not pay.

3. He offered an adequate sacrifice for sin, which we were not able to offer.

4. He met and defeated sin and the powers of evil which had mastered us and which we had not strength to overcome.

*5. He offered a perfect obedience and thus became the
New Man, undoing the results of Adam's transgression and
making possible our incorporation into a new and sinless
humanity.*

Now it will be at once apparent that Paul is not using
these images to designate five separate events or transac-
tions, or even to designate five distinct effects of one event
or transaction. Christ's act was one act, and its effect was
one effect (though with two sides: to free us from sin and
to reconcile us to God, to offer emancipation and forgiveness). The images are, certainly in part, metaphors; [11]
they represent Paul's effort, by using every analogy which
ordinary experience presented, to make vivid and clear the
reality of the salvation offered in Christ.

This is most obviously true of the first of them. "You
are bought with a price," Paul says.[12] We recognize the
absurdity of taking that sentence as a bare, literal statement of fact, although one conspicuous "theory" of the
atonement was based upon such an understanding of it.
According to that view, man was in Satan's power; Christ
came and paid a ransom to Satan, thus bringing about the
prisoner's release. It will be granted that Paul thought of
man as being in Satan's power, but the literal application
of the sentence stops there. Indeed, literally interpreted,
this item is quite incompatible with the fourth in our series
of images. According to that representation of Christ's
work, far from paying a ransom to the powers of evil, Christ
utterly vanquished them; Christ set us free not by compen-
sating or appeasing Satan but by destroying his power.
The truth is that when Paul uses the image of the ransom,

[11] So A. Deissmann, *Paul* (London: Hodder & Stoughton, 1926), pp.
167 ff., 200 ff.; Dodd, *The Epistle of Paul to the Romans*, pp. 56 ff.

[12] I Cor. 6:20; 7:23; etc. The use of the figure of the ransom is also to be
noted in Mark 10:45 (which I am unable to ascribe to Jesus himself);
Rev. 5:9 and 14:3 f.; I Pet. 1:18; II Pet. 2:1; I Tim. 2:6.

he is meaning to say something like this: "Imagine yourself a slave or captive in the hand of a hard master who has set a price upon your head far beyond anything you could ever pay. You are utterly helpless and hopeless. Then one day a stranger comes, whom you did not know and who owes you nothing; this stranger, at great loss to himself, pays the ransom and you are set free. In the same way, Christ, at the cost of an incalculable sacrifice, sets us free from the power of sin." To try to make the analogy apply at every point is to distort Paul's meaning. The same metaphorical character, I am inclined to think, is not altogether absent from Paul's use of the ideas of a penalty paid and a sacrifice offered, though here the consciously metaphorical is merging into the unconsciously mythological.

This latter character plainly belongs to the conceptions of Christ as winning a cosmic victory over sin and Satan, and as becoming the Second Adam. These two ideas are closely related and, in my judgment, have an importance for Paul and are intended with a literalism and realism which cannot be affirmed of any of the other images, although, as will soon appear, I am by no means dismissing the second and third of them as mere metaphors. We have seen that Paul interprets the human tragedy as consisting essentially in man's slavery to sin and that he thought of this slavery as following upon man's defeat by the evil powers when Adam transgressed God's command. This being true, it is not strange that he should understand the freedom from the guilt and power of sin which, he is persuaded, is now available to him and to all men who believe in Christ, as owing to the victory which the man Christ Jesus has, by his obedience "even unto death," won over man's demonic enemies. As by man came sin and death, so by man have come forgiveness and life. As Adam was the head of the old, natural humanity, which sin has marred and despoiled, so Christ is the head of a new, spiritual (that is, supernatural) humanity, in which are righteousness and peace. Salvation consists in dying to the old world and becoming alive in the new; in the breaking of contact with the order of relationships which is " Adam " and the entering into the new order of relationships which is " Christ." " As in Adam all die, even so in Christ shall all be made alive." [13]

Obviously, this conception is eschatological. The " new humanity " belongs to the new age. The " new order of relationships " is the order of the world to come. The salvation of which Paul speaks is primarily salvation within the kingdom of God which, whatever it may have been for Jesus himself, lay beyond the end of history for Paul and the primitive church. Their thinking was largely affected by Jewish apocalyptic conceptions, according to which history had fallen under the dominion of demonic powers; when " the fullness of time " should come, God would engage these powers in battle, would defeat and destroy them and their human agents, and would inaugurate a new and unimaginable order of blessedness, righteousness and peace. Clearly the conception of Christ as Victor over man's demonic enemies and as thus becoming the Second

[13] See I Cor. 15:20 ff. and Rom. 5:12 ff. The conception of Christ as having won a cosmic victory over the demonic powers on our behalf, though it is worked out more consistently and fully in Paul than elsewhere, is by no means peculiar to him. Mark all but begins his story with a reference to Jesus' struggle with the Devil in the wilderness and represents the whole career of Jesus, under one of its aspects, as a demonstration of victorious power over the demons. The same note is struck again and again in the other Synoptic Gospels. One remembers especially the saying ascribed to Jesus (in Luke 22:53) in the moment of his arrest: " This is your hour and the power of darkness." And although earlier apocalyptic conceptions are generally missing in the Fourth Gospel, as we have already had occasion to observe, traces of this idea of Christ's victory are to be found even there; as in 14:30: " Hereafter I will not talk much with you: for the prince of this world cometh and hath nothing in me "; in 16:11: " The prince of this world is judged "; and in 12:31: " Now is the judgment of this world: now shall the prince of this world be cast out."

Man, with whom we may be identified, in whom we may be incorporated, in just the same sense as we belong, as natural men, to Adam — clearly this conception fits into the apocalyptic pattern. " In Adam " we belong to this world; " in Christ " we belong to the world to come.

But this conception, while it is eschatological (and eschatological in a literal temporal sense, not in the sublimated sense in which moderns sometimes use the term), is not simply futuristic. I have already had occasion several times to refer to the fact that the primitive church (possibly even Jesus himself) believed the eschatological event had already begun to occur. The end of history was not merely to happen and to happen soon; it was then happening. According to Paul, the sentence of death has already been placed upon sin. Thus he can speak of sin as being dead in those who have " died " and " risen " with Christ — that is, those who have become members of the new social reality of which Christ is the representative Head and Center.[14] But, in the next breath, by his ethical appeals, admonitions and denunciations, he can indicate unmistakably his recognition that sin is not only not dead but is having sometimes devastating results among those who presumably have been redeemed from its power. And in that connection, one remembers his description in Romans 7:24 f. of his own experience of bondage and deliverance, both referred to in the present tense as though they were happening together.

The truth is that sin, as Paul speaks of it, is both dead and not dead; justification and new life are both present and not present. Sin is dead in the sense not only that it is doomed but that the doom is already in process of being executed: " the Wrath *is being* revealed." Justification and new life are present in the sense that they have not only been surely promised but token installments, so to

14 See, for example, Rom. 6:1 ff. and Col. 3:1 ff.

speak, have already been received. The Spirit is spoken of as the " earnest " (vastly more than a promise) of the salvation, which in its fullness is still in the future. In the same way the church might have been spoken of as the " earnest " of the kingdom. The present and the future are so close to each other that Paul and other early Christians can mix the tenses in ways impossible for us. Notice how " futures " and " presents " are interspersed in Romans 8: for example, Paul can say in verse 15 that we " have received the Spirit of adoption " and in verse 23 can speak of our " groaning within ourselves " as " we wait for the adoption." The presence of the word "Spirit" in one of these passages and in the immediate context of the other suggests the only resolution of this contradiction, if any resolution is possible. We *do* wait for the adoption — *that* will come at the fulfillment of all things, which, however imminent, is still future; but even now we possess the *Spirit* of adoption, that is, God's miraculous gift of forgiveness and grace, an advance installment, a token payment, a foretaste, a " first-fruits," of a life which in its full, true character belongs only to the world to come.

Sin is doomed and its power is weakened, but it has not been actually destroyed; salvation has already been bestowed in Christ, but the fulfillment of that salvation awaits Christ's return in glorious power to bring to completion his victory over sin and death and to inaugurate fully and finally the kingdom of God.

We are now in position to see more clearly how Paul understood the necessity of the incarnation,[15] about which we were speaking in the preceding lecture. The Son of God became man in order to meet and deal with the sin which had established itself in man's flesh. The unspeakable sac-

---

[15] This term can scarcely be avoided, but will be understood, when applied to Paul, in the light of what I tried to say above, pp. 91 ff.

rifice, the self-emptying, involved in Christ's coming, had
to be made because only within human life itself could
man's enemy be found. (Here is further proof, if any were
needed, that Paul had entire confidence in the reality of
Jesus' manhood. No pseudo-man, no half-man, could do the
work that needed to be done.) Christ entered the area
where sin was exercising its sovereignty and by his perfect
obedience to the will of God decisively defeated this demonic foe. The cross marked the moment of the foe's
most determined assault, when this obedience was most
sorely tested. Just as the Son of God had to come in the
flesh in order to meet Sin, so he had to die in order to meet
Death. The resurrection is the moment, and the seal, of
his victory. God, in Christ, suffered sinful flesh that he
might destroy Sin; he suffered death that he might destroy
Death. So much has God loved us; so much has he done
for us men and for our salvation.

Thus far in this part of our discussion I have been trying
to show that Paul's thinking about the work of Christ is
predominantly eschatological: In virtue of an obedience
which man, who stood simply in the succession of Adam,
could not give, and of a victory which man could not win,
the human situation has been radically transformed. A new
humanity has been created, the spiritual humanity of the
age to come, to which even now one can belong (fully, in
principle, and partially in actual fact), through faith in —
that is, through personal trust and self-denying devotion to
— the one who loved us and gave himself for us. Such a
one is " in Christ." He is, again in principle (but also, in
a measure, actually), released from his bondage to his old
enemies; he is dead to sin and alive to righteousness. The
church is the embodiment, the manifestation within the

present brief time, of this new humanity. It is " the body of Christ." To belong to the community is to be " in Christ "; to be " in Christ " is to belong to the community.[16] Whatever more mystical connotations this phrase " in Christ " may sometimes have in Paul,[17] its primary meaning is eschatological. It designates membership in God's new and final creation, the kingdom of God, and in the church, which is (more than the promise) the actual inbreaking of that kingdom.

But though Paul's thinking about the work of Christ is, in my judgment, primarily concerned with Christ's victory over man's demonic enemies, there is a juridical note in it which cannot be denied and must not be ignored. Paul speaks again and again of Christ as " dying for our sin." On one occasion he mentions this as an element in the faith which he had received from earlier believers,[18] and the prevalence in almost every part of the New Testament of references to Christ's death as being " for us " or " for our sins " or " for sin " confirms his statement. Such references fit better with items 2 and 3 in our list on page 118 than with item 4. They can be taken most naturally as allusions, not to a battle fought and won, but to a penalty paid or a sacrifice offered.

The vicarious penal or sacrificial value of the death of Christ is indicated also by not infrequent allusions to " the blood " of Christ. Particularly important is the reference, with its context, which appears in Romans 3:25. There, having quoted from the Psalms, " None is righteous, no, not one," Paul goes on to say:

16 Baptism can thus be described as an initiation " into Christ." See Rom. 6:3; Gal. 3:27; Col. 2:12.
17 No reader of the fourth lecture in this series will suspect me of denying the reality and importance of Paul's " Christ-mysticism." On this see A. Deissmann, *The Religion of Jesus and the Faith of Paul* (London: Hodder & Stoughton, 1923) , pp. 162 ff.
18 I Cor. 15:3.

Whatever the Law says, we know, it says to those who are inside the Law, that every mouth may be shut and all the world made answerable to God; for no person will be acquitted in his sight on the score of obedience to Law. What the Law imparts is the consciousness of sin. But now we have a righteousness of God disclosed apart from law altogether; it is attested by the Law and the prophets, but it is a righteousness of God which comes by believing in Jesus Christ. And it is meant for all who have faith. No distinctions are drawn. All have sinned, all come short of the glory of God, but they are justified for nothing by his grace through the ransom provided in Christ Jesus, whom God put forward as the means of propitiation by his blood, to be received by faith. This was to demonstrate the justice of God in view of the fact that sins previously committed during the time of God's forbearance had been passed over; it was to demonstrate his justice at the present epoch, showing that God is just himself and that he justifies man on the score of faith in Jesus.[19]

There can be no doubt that we have here an allusion to Christ's death as constituting a sacrificial offering on account of sin and a satisfaction of the demands of God's righteousness. Dodd rightly insists that the term " expiation " should be read instead of " propitiation "[20] — the situation is not that an angry God needs to be placated and that he *is* placated by the blood of an innocent victim (such an idea would have seemed monstrous: after all, it is God who is " setting forth the expiation "; it is God who is seeking to " reconcile the world to himself ") , but rather that sin needs to be covered or annulled. But even so, the passage reflects the conviction, to which I referred early in this discussion, that man not only is the slave of sin but is guilty before God. It is not enough to escape from bondage to a hated, alien foe (" a law in my members which wars against the law of my mind and brings me into captivity to the law

[19] Rom. 3:19–31. From *The Bible: A New Translation*. By James Moffatt. Harper & Brothers, Publishers. Used by permission.
[20] *The Epistle of Paul to the Romans*, pp. 54 ff.

of sin in my members ") ; something must be done about
my own ghastly guilt.

Thus, we cannot, as in the case of the " ransom," regard
Paul's images of the legal penalty and of the sacrificial offering merely as graphic metaphors, however apt. He is
not saying, " It is as though you were subject to the penalty
of death and someone freely paid that penalty for you," or
' It is as though you had committed a crime far beyond the
power of any sacrifice you could offer to expiate and someone made the adequate sacrifice on your behalf." No, the
situation is not thus hypothetical. Rather, you *are* subject
to the penalty of death — it has not only been imposed but
it is deserved; you *are* guilty beyond your power to expiate;
and yet you *are*, in Christ, forgiven. It was almost inevitable that the early church — for here the various voices of
the New Testament speak with extraordinary unanimity —
should find in the death of Christ the vicarious expiatory
significance which alone could resolve this paradox. This
understanding of the death of Christ as representing a vicarious offering to God cannot be rendered consistent within
itself (since it is God who both makes the offering and re-
ceives it) , nor can it be made logically compatible with the
conception of Christus Victor.[21] But it answers to a real
element in the Christian experience of salvation. Just as
sin is known as both guilt and bondage, so salvation is received as both expiation and deliverance.

I have just said that in this understanding of the death of
Christ as a sacrifice for sin the various writers of the New
Testament almost without exception agree. (The exceptions — some of the briefer Epistles — are not important
and, even so, may only appear to be such.) It goes almost

---

[21] But see the significant book of G. Aulén, *Christus Victor* (New York
and Toronto: Macmillan Co., 1931) , in which an attempt is made to work
out such a logical synthesis.

without saying, in view of what we observed in the preceding lecture, that at the very beginning (that is, immediately after the resurrection) Jesus' death would have had little, if any, theological significance. As the first believers saw it, the resurrection was the first really significant moment. It was then that Jesus became " Lord and Christ "; it was then that he " was installed Son of God with power." The life of Jesus preceding that exaltation was, of course, vividly remembered and was laden with the most poignant meaning, but this meaning was not, certainly in any way that could have been made explicit, theological in character. It was only after it had come to be seen that Jesus must have been the Messiah even during his earthly life (and this, we can be sure, happened almost at once) that the death became a matter for theological reflection.

At first, it must have had the aspect of a difficult problem, a " stumbling-block," as Paul later tells us it still was for the Jews. But soon it was realized — partly as a result of the remembrance of Jesus' own utter humility and denial of self, particularly as associated with his awful suffering and his uncomplaining acceptance of it as the will of God; partly under the influence of a fresh reading of the Suffering Servant passages in Isaiah; [22] and, not least, as a consequence of the community's own experience of the forgiveness of sins — soon, I say, it was realized that the whole significance of Jesus' earthly life culminated in his death. As the hour approached, his " soul was exceeding sorrowful even unto death "; and in the final agony it seemed that even God had " forsaken " him.[23] But this was no fortuitous or meaningless catastrophe: He was doing the thing he came to do. He was tasting death for every man. He was, in ways hidden in mystery, destroying the power and guilt of sin.

Here is where Paul stood, as we have seen; and he stood,

[22] See above, note on p. 39.   [23] Mark 14:34; 15:34.

in all essentials, on common ground. This feeling for the deep significance of the suffering and death of Christ is constantly present in Mark, as the quotations just above will have indicated (as well as the familiar " to give his life a ransom for many " [24]), and is only less important in Matthew and Luke-Acts. The very theme of the Epistle to the Hebrews is the sacrificial death of Christ, and I Peter and the Apocalypse are full of allusions to it. The Lord's Supper, originally Jesus' last meal with his disciples before he and they should eat and drink together in the kingdom of God,[25] becomes a memorial to his death, a communion in his body and blood, and thus a participation in the salvation made possible by his sacrifice. And though in the Fourth Gospel the notes of agonizing struggle, or even of ordinary human weakness and suffering, are muted, if not hushed, and the death is, as Vincent Taylor says, " no longer a σκάνδαλον but a shining stairway by which the Son of God ascends to his Father," [26] nevertheless it is in this Gospel that Christ is both " the good shepherd " who " giveth his life for the sheep " and the " lamb of God that taketh away the sin of the world," and it is in the closely related First Epistle of John that God is said to have " sent his son to be an expiation for our sin." [27]

[24] See F. C. Grant, *The Earliest Gospel* (New York and Nashville: Abingdon-Cokesbury Press, 1943), pp. 78 ff.

[25] See Otto, *The Kingdom of God and the Son of Man*, pp. 265 ff.

[26] *The Atonement in New Testament Teaching*, p. 215. See also Colwell, *John Defends the Gospel*, pp. 67 ff.

[27] In the Fourth Gospel the saving significance of Jesus resides rather in what he was than in anything he did. Therefore all that was said in the preceding lecture about that Gospel's understanding of the nature of Christ throws light upon its understanding of his work. We have already noted in the Fourth Gospel traces of the earlier apocalyptic notion of a victorious conflict with the powers of this world and now we are observing indications of the conception of Christ's death as sacrifice for sin. But the primary significance of Christ for the author of this Gospel lies in his having been the manifestation of the Father, the incarnation of the Son of God. Christ came not primarily to *do* something (as in Paul), but to reveal something. We are saved through the appropriation of this revela-

The use of this penal and sacrificial imagery reflects the early church's profound sense of guilt, and its knowledge, which seemed to have come to it by way of the spectacle of Christ's sufferings, that the forgiveness which it now enjoyed, although given freely had not been given lightly. God had not ignored man's guilt; he had *forgiven* it. All forgiveness is costly; and God's forgiveness, it was instinctively known, had cost infinitely. Involved in the " conviction of sin " is the realization that God takes sin with immeasurably more seriousness than even the most repentant sinner can. The death of Christ became the awesome symbol of God's inescapable judgment upon sin. God's forgiveness of our sin, it was felt, did not cost him his righteousness only because it had cost him his Son.

But if this gift of his Son was, in some way beyond the early church's or our own understanding, a satisfaction of God's justice, it was even more manifestly an expression of his love. If the death of Christ spoke of God's judgment, it spoke also of his mercy. Indeed, the wonder of the cross was that it revealed a righteousness in which justice and love were finally one. It is because God is love that our rebellion against his righteous will is so utterly appalling. It is precisely because God is forgiving that our sin is so heinous. Thus the recognition of the forgiveness of God, far from mitigating our awareness of judgment, serves immeasurably to deepen it. The more gracious God is, the more terrible our disobedience and disloyalty. The cross, in forcing us to face the tragic facts of our sin and of God's judgment on it, confronts us also inescapably with the love of God, and thus with the deepest and most tragic meaning of our sin.

The realization of that deepest meaning is repentance.

---

tion, for salvation, or " eternal life," is the knowledge of, the fellowship with, God which was made possible by the manifestation among men of the Eternal Word and is still possible in the church through the Spirit, which, as we have seen, is Christ's continuing presence.

One may, in other ways, feel sorrow for sin (the sorrow of regret, or remorse, or despair) ; but one cannot feel the sorrow of repentance (which alone leads to forgiveness and salvation) unless one knows that God suffers because of our sin incalculably more than we — and that he suffers willingly and out of love for us. The sorrow of repentance grows out of a recognition that we have not only transgressed the law of God but have brought grief to the love of God. But this same love stands ready to redeem us. The very love which drives us to the verge of despair when we think of what we have done to it, grasps us at the edge of the precipice and brings us home again. " O wretched man that I am! Who will deliver me? I thank God through Jesus Christ our Lord! "

So much for an attempt to interpret several important strains in early Christian reflection upon the significance of Jesus. I should like to conclude by emphasizing again the distinction between Christ and Christology, and by insisting once more that Christ is more important than Christology, as life is more important than dogma. By " Christ " we mean the One remembered and still known in the church, by whom we are grasped, through whom we are forgiven, in whom we have been found of God. By " Christology " we mean the attempts of the church to explain this Reality. The two are closely related but are not identical. One can know Christ and " the power of his resurrection " without finding entirely congenial any of the classical interpretations of that experience. Indeed, such a one is certain to feel that none of these interpretations is altogether adequate; and some of them he will reject (whether he knows he is doing so or not) as quite useless.

And yet few things are more certain than that the church

will never find it possible to reject or replace the more *important* terms with which the last two lectures have abounded — terms like the creation and the fall of man and the coming and the dying of the Son of God. This is true not because the church will necessarily feel itself bound by these terms (we are not to feel bound by any terms: God has not called us to bondage, but to freedom), but because what these terms stand for cannot be translated into the language either of ordinary speech or of scientific and philosophical discourse. What is said by such statements as " Christ died for us," or " God sent his son into the world that the world through him might be saved," or " God was in Christ reconciling the world unto himself " cannot be said otherwise.

The reason the basic and common christological terms will always prove to be both indispensable and irreplaceable is that they stand, as mythological terms invariably do, not primarily for abstract ideas, but for concrete realities known within the experience of the community — the realities dealt with in the first three, and particularly in the fourth, of these lectures. Indeed, such conceptions as Christ's victory over sin and death on our behalf and the forgiveness of sins through him are part and parcel of the event itself which we know as Jesus Christ. To this extent Christology is inseparable from Christ.

Just as it would be impossible to replace with definitions such words as " home," or " light," or " music," or to make the meaning of such words clear to someone who had never himself experienced the realities to which they point, so it will always be impossible to replace with definitions such terms as " the grace of God in Christ," " peace with God through our Lord Jesus Christ," or the great story in which these phrases have their only possible context. Definitions and explanations will often be of the greatest value, but they will never exhaust the meaning of the realities within the life of the church to which these terms refer nor will they render the terms themselves unnecessary. Particular terms we may discard; but in so far as the New Testament story as a whole has fallen into disuse, it is not because we are too intelligent to believe it but because we are too small and poor to know what it means.

Those to whom, all unworthy, the suffering and forgiving love of God has been revealed in Christ will find themselves, in every generation, laying eager hold upon the terms which sprang out of the experience of the first recipients of this revelation. Those to whom it has been given to see the glory of God in the face of Jesus Christ will gladly claim the words in which the first wondering witnesses expressed their rapture and their awe. They will know that whatever may be the real and ultimate truth of God's being and purpose (and it must be, in the nature of the case, far beyond our knowing), we never approach so near to that truth as when we say with Paul, " God commendeth his love toward us, in that, while we were yet sinners, Christ died for us," or with the author of the Fourth Gospel, " God so loved the world that he gave his only begotten son," or with still another of those upon whom the light first shone, " Because of the great love wherewith he hath loved us, God hath made us, who were dead in sins, to live again with Christ."

A Bibliography

The fact that these lectures have dealt with selected themes in a broad field puts any attempt at an exhaustive list of relevant books out of the question. In the following I have tried to include books to which I have been particularly indebted as well as a number of works which will help fill in some of the gaps which this volume obviously leaves altogether open. Translated German and French works are cited only in the English editions. I have not included the titles of articles or short essays.

AULÉN, G. *Christus Victor*. Toronto and New York: Macmillan Co., 1931.

BACON, B. W. *Jesus the Son of God*. New Haven: Yale University Press, 1911.

BAILLIE, J. *The Place of Jesus Christ in Modern Christianity*. New York: Charles Scribner's Sons, 1929.

BARNIKOL, E. *Mensch und Messias, der nichtpaulinische Ursprung der Präexistenzchristologie*. Kiel, 1932.

BEBLAVY, J. *Les Idées eschatologiques de Saint Paul et des Pères Apostoliques*. Alençon, 1924.

BELL, G. K. A., and DEISSMANN, A. *Mysterium Christi*. London and New York: Longmans, Green & Co., 1930.

BEYSCHLAG, W. *New Testament Theology*. Edinburgh: T. & T. Clark, 1895.

BOUSSET, W. *Kyrios Christos*. Göttingen, 1913.

BRANSCOMB, B. H. *The Teaching of Jesus*. Nashville: Abingdon-Cokesbury Press, 1931.

———. *The Gospel of Mark*. London and New York: Harper & Brothers, 1937.

BRÜCKNER, M. *Die Entstehung der paulinischen Christologie*. Strassburg, 1903.

CADBURY, H. J. *The Peril of Modernizing Jesus.* New York: Macmillan Co., 1937.

CADOUX, C. J. *The Historic Mission of Jesus.* London, 1941; New York: Harper & Brothers, 1943.

CARRÉ, H. B. *Paul's Doctrine of Redemption.* London and New York: Macmillan Co., 1914.

CASE, S. J. *Jesus: A New Biography.* Chicago: University of Chicago Press, 1927.

——. *Jesus Through the Centuries.* Chicago: University of Chicago Press, 1932.

CAVE, S. *The Doctrine of the Person of Christ.* New York: Charles Scribner's Sons, 1925.

——. *The Doctrine of the Work of Christ.* Nashville: Abingdon-Cokesbury Press, 1937.

COLWELL, E. C. *John Defends the Gospel.* Chicago: Willett, Clark & Co., 1936.

CRAIG, C. T. *The Beginning of Christianity.* New York: Abingdon-Cokesbury Press, 1943.

DEISSMANN, A. *The Religion of Jesus and the Faith of Paul.* London: Hodder & Stoughton, 1923.

DENNEY, J. *The Death of Christ.* New York: A. C. Armstrong & Son, 1903.

——. *Jesus and the Gospel.* New York: A. C. Armstrong & Son, 1909.

DIBELIUS, M. *Gospel Criticism and Christology.* London: J. Nicholson & Watson, 1935.

——. *The Sermon on the Mount.* New York: Charles Scribner's Sons, 1940.

DOBSCHÜTZ, E. VON. *The Eschatology of the Gospels.* London: Hodder & Stoughton, 1910.

DODD, C. H. *The Apostolic Preaching.* Chicago: Willett, Clark & Co., 1937.

——. *The Parables of the Kingdom.* New York: Charles Scribner's Sons, 1936.

——. *History and the Gospel.* London and New York: Charles Scribner's Sons, 1938.

EASTON, B. S. *Christ in the Gospels.* London and New York: Charles Scribner's Sons, 1930.

ENSLIN, M. S. *Christian Beginnings.* New York: Harper & Brothers, 1938.

FEINE, P. *Theologie des Neuen Testaments.* Leipzig, 1931.

FOAKES-JACKSON, F. J., and LAKE, KIRSOPP. *Beginnings of Christianity.* Part I, Vol. I. London: Macmillan Co., 1920.

GARDNER-SMITH, P. *The Christ of the Gospels.* Cambridge, Eng.: W. Heffer & Sons, 1938.

GILBERT, G. H. *The First Interpreters of Jesus.* New York: Macmillan Co., 1901.

GOGUEL, M. *Jesus the Nazarene.* London and New York: D. Appleton & Co., 1926.

GRANBERY, J. C. *Outline of New Testament Christology.* Chicago: University of Chicago Press, 1909.

GRANT, F. C. *The Gospel of the Kingdom.* New York: Macmillan Co., 1940.

——. *The Earliest Gospel.* New York: Abingdon-Cokesbury Press, 1943.

HARNACK, A. *History of Dogma.* London, 1894.

HÉRING, J. *Le Royaume de Dieu et sa venue.* Paris, 1937.

HOLTZMANN, H. J. *Lehrbuch der neutestamentlichen Theologie.* Freiburg, 1897.

HORTON, W. *Our Eternal Contemporary.* New York: Harper & Brothers, 1942.

KENNEDY, H. A. A. *The Theology of the Epistles.* New York: Charles Scribner's Sons, 1920.

KLAUSNER, J. *Jesus of Nazareth.* New York: Macmillan Co., 1925.

——. *From Jesus to Paul.* New York: Macmillan Co., 1943.

KRAELING, C. H. *Anthropos and Son of Man.* New York: Columbia University Press, 1927.

LIETZMANN, H. *Der Menschensohn.* Freiburg and Leipzig, 1896.

LIGHTFOOT, R. H. *History and Interpretation in the Gospels.* New York: Harper & Brothers, 1935.

McCOWN, C. C. *The Search for the Real Jesus.* New York: Charles Scribner's Sons, 1940.

McGIFFERT, A. C. *History of Christian Thought.* New York: Charles Scribner's Sons, 1932.

MACKINNON, J. *The Historic Jesus.* London and New York: Longmans, Green & Co., 1931.

——. *The Gospel of the Early Church.* London: Longmans, Green & Co., 1933.

MACKINTOSH, H. R. *The Doctrine of the Person of Christ.* New York: Charles Scribner's Sons, 1912.

McNEILE, A. H. *New Testament Teaching in the Light of St. Paul's.* New York: Macmillan Co., 1923.

MacNEILL, H. L. *The Christology of the Epistle to the Hebrews.* Chicago: University of Chicago Press, 1914.

MANSON, T. W. *The Teaching of Jesus.* Cambridge, Eng.: Cambridge University Press, 1931.

MANSON, W. *Jesus the Messiah.* London: Hodder & Stoughton, 1943.

———. *Christ's View of the Kingdom of God.* London: James Clark & Co., 1918.

MATHEWS, S. *Messianic Hope in the New Testament.* Chicago: University of Chicago Press, 1905.

MINEAR, P. S. *And Great Shall Be Your Reward.* New Haven: Yale University Press, 1941.

MOFFATT, J. *The Theology of the Gospels.* London, 1912; New York: Charles Scribner's Sons, 1913.

MORGAN, W. *The Religion and Theology of Paul.* Edinburgh: T. & T. Clark, 1917.

MORRISON, C. C. *What Is Christianity?* Chicago: Willett, Clark & Co., 1940.

OTTO, R. *The Kingdom of God and the Son of Man.* London and Grand Rapids, Mich.: Zondervan Publishing House, 1938-39.

PFLEIDERER, O. *The Early Christian Conception of Christ.* London: Williams & Norgate, 1905; New York: G. P. Putnam's Sons, 1905.

———. *Paulinism.* London: Williams & Norgate, 1877 and 1891.

PITTENGER, W. N. *Christ and Christian Faith.* New York: Round Table Press, 1941.

PORTER, F. C. *The Mind of Christ in Paul.* New York: Charles Scribner's Sons, 1930.

RASHDALL, H. *The Idea of Atonement in Christian Theology.* London and New York: Macmillan Co., 1920.

RAWLINSON, A. E. J. *The New Testament Doctrine of Christ.* London: Longmans, Green & Co., 1926.

ROBERTS, D. E., and VAN DUSEN, H. P., eds. *Liberal Theology.* New York: Charles Scribner's Sons, 1942. See especially the essay by Van Dusen, "The Significance of Jesus Christ."

SANDAY, W. *Christologies Ancient and Modern.* New York: Oxford University Press, 1910.

SCHWEITZER, A. *The Mystery of the Kingdom.* New York: Dodd, Mead & Co., 1914.

———. *The Quest of the Historical Jesus.* London: A. & C. Black, 1910.

———. *The Mysticism of Paul the Apostle.* London: A. & C. Black, 1931.

SCOTT, C. A. A. *Christianity according to Paul.* Cambridge, Eng.: Cambridge University Press, 1927.

SCOTT, E. F. *The Kingdom and the Messiah.* Edinburgh: T. & T. Clark, 1911.

———. *The Fourth Gospel.* Edinburgh: T. & T. Clark, 1908.

———. *The New Testament Idea of Revelation.* New York: Charles Scribner's Sons, 1935.

———. *The Nature of the Early Church.* New York: Charles Scribner's Sons, 1941.

SELLARS, R. V. *Two Ancient Christologies.* London: Society for the Promotion of Christian Knowledge, 1940.

SHARMAN, H. B. *Son of Man and Kingdom of God.* New York: Harper & Brothers, 1943.

SIMKHOVITCH, V. G. *Toward the Understanding of Jesus.* New York: Macmillan Co., 1921.

SMART, W. A. *The Contemporary Christ.* Nashville: Abingdon-Cokesbury Press, 1943.

STRACHAN, R. H. *The Historic Jesus in the New Testament.* London: Student Christian Movement Press, 1931.

TAYLOR, V. *The Atonement in New Testament Teaching.* London: Epworth Press, 1940.

———. *Jesus and His Sacrifice.* London: Macmillan Co., 1937.

THACKERAY, H. ST. J. *The Relation of St. Paul to Contemporary Jewish Thought.* London: Macmillan Co., 1900.

WEINEL, H. *Biblische Theologie des Neuen Testaments.* Tübingen, 1911.

WEISS, B. *Biblical Theology of the New Testament.* Edinburgh: T. & T. Clark, 1879.

WEISS, J. *Paul and Jesus.* New York: Harper & Brothers, 1909.
————. *Christ: the Beginnings of Dogma.* Boston: Beacon Press, 1911.
————. *History of Primitive Christianity.* New York: Wilson-Erickson, Inc., 1937.
WILDER, A. N. *Eschatology and Ethics in the Teaching of Jesus.* New York: Harper & Brothers, 1939.
WINDISCH, H. *Der Sinn der Bergpredigt.* Leipzig, 1929.
WREDE, W. *Paulus.* Tübingen, 1907.
————. *Das Messiasgeheimnis in den Evangelien.* Göttingen, 1901.

INDEXES

Scripture and Other Sources

Authors

Subjects